Elements: Great Essays

Edited by John Pfannkuchen.

Original essays by respective authors, edited for readability.

Copyright © 2019 by Elwood Learning

Elwood Learning

32 Terrace Dr

Binghamton, NY 13905

www.elwoodlearning.com

Ordering Information: Quantity sales. Special discounts are available on quantity purchases by corporations, associations, and others. For details, contact the publisher at the address above.

Orders by U.S. trade bookstores and wholesalers. Please contact Ingram Distribution at

One Ingram Blvd.,

La Vergne, TN 37086

615.793.5000

Printed in the United States of America. Published by Elwood Learning, an imprint of Elwood Publishing.

D1316663

ELEMENTS: GREAT ESSAYS

On Railways and Things

Hilaire Belloc

1   Railways have changed the arrangement and distribution of crowds and solitude, but have done nothing to disturb the essential contrast between them.

2   The more behindhand of my friends, among whom I count the weary men of the towns, are ceaselessly bewailing the effect of railways and the spoiling of the country; nor do I fail, when I hear such complaints, to point out their error, courteously to hint at their sheep-like qualities, and with all the delicacy imaginable to let them understand they are no better than machines repeating worn-out formulae through the nose. The railways and those slow lumbering things the steamboats have not spoilt our solitudes, on the contrary they have intensified the quiet of the older haunts, they have created new sanctuaries, and (crowning blessing) they make it easy for us to reach our refuges.

3   For in the first place you will notice that new lines of travel are like canals cut through the stagnant marsh of an old civilisation, draining it of populace and worry, and concentrating upon themselves the odious pressure of humanity.

4   You know (to adopt the easy or conversational style) that you and I belong to a happy minority. We are the sons of the hunters and the wandering singers, and from our boyhood nothing ever gave us greater pleasure than to stand under lonely skies in forest clearings, or to find a beach looking westward at evening over unfrequented seas. But the great mass of men love companionship so much that nothing seems of any worth compared with it. Human communion is their meat and drink, and so they use the railways to make bigger and bigger hives for themselves.

5   Now take the true modern citizen, the usurer. How does the usurer suck the extremest pleasure out of his holiday? He takes the train

preferably at a very central station near the Strand, and (if he can choose his time) on a foggy and dirty day; he picks out an express that will take him with the greatest speed through the Garden of Eden, nor does he begin to feel the full savour of relaxation till a row of abominable villas' appears on the southern slope of what were once the downs; these villas stand like the skirmishers of a foul army deployed: he is immediately whirled into Brighton and is at peace. There he has his wish for three days; there he can never see anything but houses, or, if he has to walk along the sea, he can rest his eye on herds of unhappy people and huge advertisements, and he can hear the newspaper boys telling lies (perhaps special lies he has paid for) at the top of their voices; he can note as evening draws on the pleasant glare of gas upon the street mud and there pass him the familiar surroundings of servility, abject poverty, drunkenness, misery, and vice. He has his music-hall on the Saturday evening with the sharp, peculiar finish of the London accent in the patriotic song, he has the London paper on Sunday to tell him that his nastiest little Colonial War was a crusade, and on Monday morning he has the familiar feeling that follows his excesses of the previous day.... Are you not glad that such men and their lower-fellows swarm by hundreds of thousands into the "resorts"? Do you not bless the railways that take them so quickly from one Hell to another.

6   Never let me hear you say that the railways spoil a countryside; they do, it is true, spoil this or that particular place—as, for example, Crewe, Brighton, Stratford-on-Avon—but for this disadvantage they give us I know not how many delights. What is more English than the country railway station? I defy the eighteenth century to produce anything more English, more full of home and rest and the nature of the country, than my junction. Twenty-seven trains a day stop at it or start from it; it serves even the expresses. Smith's monopoly has a bookstall there; you can get cheap Kipling and Harmsworth to any extent, and yet it is a theme for English

idylls. The one-eyed porter whom I have known from childhood; the station-master who ranges us all in ranks, beginning with the Duke and ending with a sad, frayed and literary man; the little chaise in which the two old ladies from Barlton drive up to get their paper of an evening, the servant from the inn, the newsboy whose mother keeps a sweetshop—they are all my village friends. The glorious Sussex accent, whose only vowel is the broad "a", grows but more rich and emphatic from the necessity of impressing itself upon foreign intruders. The smoke also of the train as it skirts the Downs is part and parcel of what has become (thanks to the trains) our encloistered country life; the smoke of the trains is a little smudge of human activity which permits us to match our incomparable seclusion with the hurly-burly from which we have fled. Upon my soul, when I climb up the Beacon to read my book on the warm turf, the sight of an engine coming through the cutting is an emphasis of my selfish enjoyment. I say "There goes the Brighton train", but the image of Brighton, with its Anglo-Saxons and its Vision of Empire, does not oppress me; it is a far-off thing; its life ebbs and flows along that belt of iron to distances that do not regard me.

7 Consider this also with regard to my railway: it brings me what I want in order to be perfect in my isolation. Those books discussing Problems: whether or not there is such an idea as right; the inconvenience of being married; the worry of being Atheist and yet living upon a clerical endowment,—these fine discussions come from a library in a box by train and I can torture myself for a shilling, whereas, before the railways, I should have had to fall back on the Gentleman's Magazine and the County History. In the way of newspapers it provides me with just the companionship necessary to a hermitage. Often and often, after getting through one paper, I stroll down to the junction and buy fifteen others, and so enjoy the fruits of many minds.

8 Thanks to my railway I can sit in the garden of an evening and read

my paper as I smoke my pipe, and say, "Ah! That's Buggin's work. I remember him well; he worked for Rhodes…. Hullo! Here's Simpson at it again; since when did they buy him? …" And so forth. I lead my pastoral life, happy in the general world about me, and I serve, as sauce to such healthy meat, the piquant wickedness of the town; nor do I ever note a cowardice, a lie, a bribery, or a breach of trust, a surrender in the field, or a new Peerage, but I remember that my newspaper could not add these refining influences to my life but for the railway which I set out to praise at the beginning of this and intend to praise manfully to the end.

9 Yet another good we owe to railways occurs to me. They keep the small towns going.

10 Don't pester me with "economics" on that point; I know more economics than you, and I say that but for the railways the small towns would have gone to pieces. There never yet was a civilisation growing richer and improving its high roads in which the small towns did not dwindle. The village supplied the local market with bodily necessaries; the intellectual life, the civic necessities had to go into the large towns. It happened in the second and third centuries in Italy; it happened in France between Henri IV and the Revolution; it was happening here before 1830.

11 Take those little paradises Ludlow and Leominster; consider Arundel, and please your memory with the admirable slopes of Whitchurch; grow contented in a vision of Ledbury, of Rye, or of Abingdon, or of Beccles with its big church over the river, or of Newport in the Isle of Wight, or of King's Lynn, or of Lymington—you would not have any of these but for the railway, and there are 1800 such in England—one for every tolerable man.

12 Valognes in the Cotentin, Bourg-d'Oysan down in the Dauphiné in its vast theatre of upright hills, St. Julien in the Limousin, Aubusson-in-the-hole, Puy (who does not connect beauty with the word?), Mansle in the Charente country—they had all been half dead for over a century when the railway came to them and made

them jolly, little, trim, decent, self-contained, worthy, satisfactory, genial, comforting and human [Greek: politeiae], with clergy, upper class, middle class, poor, soldiers, yesterday's news, a college, anti-Congo men, fools, strong riders, old maids, and all that makes a state. In England the railway brought in that beneficent class, the gentlemen; in France, that still more beneficent class, the Haute Bourgeoisie.

13 I know what you are going to say; you are going to say that there were squires before the railways in England. Pray have you considered how many squires there were to go round? About half a dozen squires to every town, that is (say) four gentlemen, and of those four gentlemen let us say two took some interest in the place. It wasn't good enough ... and heaven help the country towns now if they had to depend on the great houses! There would be a smart dog-cart once a day with a small (vicious and servile) groom in it, an actor, a foreign money-lender, a popular novelist, or a newspaper owner jumping out to make his purchases and driving back again to his host's within the hour. No, no; what makes the country town is the Army, the Navy, the Church, and the Law—especially the retired ones.

14 Then think of the way in which the railways keep a good man's influence in a place and a bad man's out of it. Your good man loves a country town, but he must think, and read, and meet people, so in the last century he regretfully took a town house and had his little house in the country as well. Now he lives in the country and runs up to town when he likes.

15 He is always a permanent influence in the little city—especially if he has but £400 a year, which is the normal income of a retired gentleman (yes, it is so, and if you think it is too small an estimate, come with me some day and make an inquisitorial tour of my town). As for the vulgar and cowardly man, he hates small towns (fancy a South African financier in a small town!), well, the railway takes him away. Of old he might have had to stay there or starve,

now he goes to London and runs a rag, or goes into Parliament, or goes to dances dressed up in imitation of a soldier; or he goes to Texas and gets hanged—it's all one to me. He's out of my town.

16 And as the railways have increased the local refinement and virtue, so they have ennobled and given body to the local dignitary. What would the Bishop of Caen (he calls himself Bishop of Lisieux and Bayeux, but that is archaeological pedantry); what, I say, would the Bishop of Caen be without his railway? A Phantom or a Paris magnate. What the Mayor of High Wycombe? Ah! what indeed! But I cannot waste any more of this time of mine in discussing one aspect of the railway; what further I have to say on the subject shall be presented in due course in my book on The Small Town of Christendom [Footnote: The Small Town of Christendom: an Analytical Study. With an Introduction by Joseph Reinach. Ulmo et Cie. £25 nett.] I will close this series of observations with a little list of benefits the railway gives you, many of which would not have occurred to you but for my ingenuity, some of which you may have thought of at some moment or other, and yet would never have retained but for my patient labour in this.

17 The railway gives you seclusion. If you are in an express alone you are in the only spot in Western Europe where you can be certain of two or three hours to yourself. At home in the dead of night you may be wakened by a policeman or a sleep-walker or a dog. The heaths are populous. You cannot climb to the very top of Helvellyn to read your own poetry to yourself without the fear of a tourist. But in the corner of a third-class going north or west you can be sure of your own company; the best, the most sympathetic, the most brilliant in the world.

18 The railway gives you sharp change. And what we need in change is surely keenness. For instance, if one wanted to go sailing in the old days, one left London, had a bleak drive in the country, got nearer and nearer the sea, felt the cold and wet and discomfort growing on one, and after half a day or a day's gradual introduction to the

thing, one would at last have got on deck, wet and wretched, and half the fun over. Nowadays what happens? Why, the other day, a rich man was sitting in London with a poor friend; they were discussing what to do in three spare days they had. They said "let us sail." They left London in a nice warm, comfortable, rich-padded, swelly carriage at four, and before dark they were letting everything go, putting on the oilies, driving through the open in front of it under a treble-reefed storm jib, praying hard for their lives in last Monday's gale, and wishing to God they had stayed at home—all in the four hours. That is what you may call piquant, it braces and refreshes a man.

19 For the rest I cannot detail the innumerable minor advantages of railways; the mild excitement which is an antidote to gambling; the shaking which (in moderation) is good for livers; the meeting familiarly with every kind of man and talking politics to him; the delight in rapid motion; the luncheon-baskets; the porters; the solid guard; the strenuous engine-driver (note this next time you travel—it is an accurate observation). And of what other kind of modern thing can it be said that more than half pay dividends? Thinking of these things, what sane and humorous man would ever suggest that a part of life, so fertile in manifold and human pleasure, should ever be bought by the dull clique who call themselves "the State", and should yield under such a scheme yet more, yet larger, yet securer salaries to the younger sons.

» (1907)

Experience

Arthur Benson

1   It is very strange to contemplate the steady plunge of good advice,
like a cataract of ice-cold water, into the brimming and dancing
pool of youth and life, the maxims of moralists and sages, the
epigrams of cynics, the sermons of priests, the good-humoured
warnings of sensible men, all crying out that nothing is really worth
the winning, that fame brings weariness and anxiety, that love is a
fitful fever, that wealth is a heavy burden, that ambition is a hectic
dream; to all of which ejaculations youth does not listen and cannot
listen, but just goes on its eager way, trying its own experiments,
believing in the delight of triumph and success, determined, at all
events, to test all for itself. All this confession of disillusionment
and disappointment is true, but only partially true. The struggle,
the effort, the perseverance, does bring fine things with it—things
finer by far than the shining crown and the loud trumpets that
attend it.

2   The explanation of it seems to be that men require to be tempted to
effort, by the dream of fame and wealth and leisure and imagined
satisfaction. It is the experience that we need, though we do not
know it; and experience, by itself, seems such a tedious, dowdy,
tattered thing, like a flag burnt by sun, bedraggled by rain, torn by
the onset, that it cannot by itself prove attractive. Men are heavily
preoccupied with ends and aims, and the recognized values of the
objects of desire and hope are often false and distorted values. So
singularly constituted are we, that the hope of idleness is alluring,
and some people are early deceived into habits of idleness, because
they cannot know what it is that lies on the further side of work.
Of course the bodily life has to be supplied, but when a man has all
that he needs—let us say food and drink, a quiet shelter, a garden
and a row of trees, a grassy meadow with a flowing stream, a congenial task, a household of his own—it seems not enough! Let us

suppose all that granted to a man: he must consider next what kind of life he has gained; he has the cup in his hands; with what liquor is it to be filled? That is the point at which the imagination of man seems to fail; he cannot set himself to vigorous, wholesome life for its own sake. He has to be ever looking past it and beyond it for something to yield him an added joy.

3   Now, what we all have to do, if we can, is to regard life steadily and generously, to see that life, experience, emotion, are the real gifts; not things to be hurried through, thrust aside, disregarded, as a man makes a hasty meal before some occasion that excites him. One must not use life like the Passover feast, to be eaten with loins girded and staff in hand. It is there to be lived, and what we have to do is to make the quality of it as fine as we can.

4   We must provide then, if we can, a certain setting for life, a sufficiency of work and sustenance, and even leisure; and then we must give that no further thought. How many men do I not know, whose thought seems to be "when I have made enough money, when I have found my place, when I have arranged the apparatus of life about me, then I will live as I should wish to live." But the stream of desires broadens and thickens, and the leisure hour never comes!

5   We must not thus deceive ourselves. What we have to do is to make life, instantly and without delay, worthy to be lived. We must try to enjoy all that we have to do, and take care that we do not do what we do not enjoy, unless the hard task we set ourselves is sure to bring us something that we really need. It is useless thus to elaborate the cup of life, if we find when we have made it, that the wine which should have filled it has long ago evaporated.

6   Can I say what I believe the wine of life to be? I believe that it is a certain energy and richness of spirit, in which both mind and heart find full expression. We ought to rise day by day with a certain zest, a clear intention, a design to make the most out of every hour; not to let the busy hours shoulder each other, tread on each other's heels, but to force every action to give up its strength and sweet-

ness. There is work to be done, and there are empty hours to be filled as well. It is happiest of all, for man and woman, if those hours can be filled, not as a duty but as a pleasure, by pleasing those whom we love and whose nearness is at once a delight. We ought to make time for that most of all. And then there ought to be some occupation, not enforced, to which we naturally wish to return. Exercise, gardening, handicraft, writing, even if it be only leisurely letters, music, reading—something to occupy the restless brain and hand; for there is no doubt that both physically and mentally we are not fit to be unoccupied.

7 But most of all, there must be something to quicken, enliven, practice the soul. We must not force this upon ourselves, or it will be fruitless and dreary; but neither must we let it lapse out of mere indolence. We must follow some law of beauty, in whatever way beauty appeals to us and calls us. We must not think that appeal a selfish thing, because it is upon that and that alone that our power of increasing peace and hope and vital energy belongs.

8 I have a man in mind who has a simple taste for books. He has a singularly pure and fine power of selecting and loving what is best in books. There is no self-consciousness about him, no critical contempt of the fancies of others; but his own love for what is beautiful is so modest, so perfectly natural and unaffected, that it is impossible to hear him speak of the things that he loves without a desire rising up in one's mind to taste a pleasure which brings so much happiness to the owner. I have often talked with him about books that I had thought tiresome and dull; but he disentangles so deftly the underlying idea of the book, the thought that one must be on the look-out for the motive of the whole, that he has again and again sent me back to a book which I had thrown aside, with an added interest and perception. But the really notable thing is the effect on his own immediate circle. I do not think his family are naturally people of very high intelligence or ability. But his mind and heart seem to have permeated theirs, so that I know no group

of persons who seem to have imbibed so simply, without strain or effort, a delight in what is good and profound. There is no sort of dryness about the atmosphere. It is not that they keep talk resolutely on their own subjects; it is merely that their outlook is so fresh and quick that everything seems alive and significant. One comes away from the house with a horizon strangely extended, and a sense that the world is full of live ideas and wonderful affairs.

9   I despair of describing an effect so subtle, so contagious. It is not in the least that everything becomes intellectual; that would be a rueful consequence; there is no parade of knowledge, but knowledge itself becomes an exciting and entertaining thing, like a varied landscape. The wonder is, when one is with these people, that one did not see all the fine things that were staring one in the face all the time, the clues, the connections, the links. The best of it is that it is not a transient effect; it is rather like the implanting of a seed of fire, which spreads and glows, and burns unaided.

10   It is this sacred fire of which we ought all to be in search. Fire is surely the most wonderful symbol in the world! We sit in our quiet rooms, feeling safe, serene, even chilly, yet everywhere about us, peacefully confined in all our furniture and belongings, is a mass of inflammability, stored with gases, which at a touch are capable of leaping into flame. I remember once being in a house in which a pile of wood in a cellar had caught fire; there was a short delay, while the hose was got out, and before an aperture into the burning room could be made. I went into a peaceful dining-room, which was just above the fire, and it was strangely appalling to see little puffs of smoke fly off from the kindled floor, while we tore the carpets up and flew to take the pictures down, and to know the room was all crammed with vehement cells, ready to burst into vapour at the fierce touch of the consuming element.

11   I saw once a vast bonfire of wood kindled on a grassy hill-top; it was curiously affecting to see the great trunks melt into flame, and the red cataract pouring so softly, so unapproachably into the air. It

is so with the minds of men; the material is all there, compressed, welded, inflammable; and if the fire can but leap into our spirits from some other burning heart, we may be amazed at the prodigal force and heat that can burst forth, the silent energy, the possibility of consumption.

12 I hold it to be of supreme value to each of us to try to introduce this fire of the heart into our spirits. It is not like mortal fire, a consuming, dangerous, truculent element. It is rather like the furnace of the engine, which can convert water into steam—the softest, feeblest, purest element into irresistible and irrepressible force. The materials are all at hand in many a spirit that has never felt the glowing contact; and it is our business first to see that the elements are there, and then to receive with awe the fiery touch. It must be restrained, controlled, guarded, that fierce conflagration; but our joy cannot only consist of pure, clear, lambent, quiescent elements. It must have a heart of flame.

» (1922)

Of Death

Thomas Browne

1 This is that dismal conquest we all deplore, that makes us so often cry, O Adam, quid fecisti? ["What have you done?"]. I thank God I have not those strait ligaments, or narrow obligations to the world, as to dote on life, or be convulsed and tremble at the name of death.

2 Not that I am insensible of the dread and horror thereof; or, by raking into the bowels of the deceased, continual sight of anatomies, skeletons, or cadaverous relicks, like vespilloes, or gravemakers, I am become stupid, or have forgot the apprehension of mortality; but that, marshalling all the horrors, and contemplating the extremities thereof, I find not anything therein able to daunt the courage of a man, much less a well-resolved Christian; and therefore am not angry at the error of our first parents, or unwilling to bear a part of this common fate, and, like the best of them, to die; that is, to cease to breathe, to take a farewell of the elements; to be a kind of nothing for a moment; to be within one instant of a spirit.

3 When I take a full view and circle of myself without this reasonable moderator, and equal piece of justice, death, I do conceive myself the miserablest person extant. Were there not another life that I hope for, all the vanities of this world should not entreat a moment's breath from me.

4 Could the devil work my belief to imagine I could never die, I would not outlive that very thought. I have so abject a conceit of this common way of existence, this retaining to the sun and elements, I cannot think this is to be a man, or to live according to the dignity of humanity. In expectation of a better, I can with patience embrace this life; yet, in my best meditations, do often defy death.

5 I honour any man that condemns it; nor can I highly love any that is afraid of it: this makes me naturally love a soldier, and honour those tattered and contemptible regiments, that will die at the command of a sergeant. For a pagan there may be some motives to be in love with life; but, for a Christian to be amazed at death, I see not how he can escape this dilemma—that he is too sensible of this life, or hopeless of the life to come.

» (1642)

Of Affection

Thomas Browne

1   There are wonders in true affection. It is a body of enigmas, mysteries, and riddles; wherein two so become one as they both become two: I love my friend before myself, and yet, methinks, I do not love him enough. Some few months hence, my multiplied affection will make me believe I have not loved him at all. When I am from him, I am dead till I be with him. United souls are not satisfied with embraces, but desire to be truly each other; which being impossible, these desires are infinite, and must proceed without a possibility of satisfaction. Another misery there is in affection; that whom we truly love like our own selves, we forget their looks, nor can our memory retain the idea of their faces: and it is no wonder, for they are ourselves, and our affection makes their looks our own. This noble affection falls not on vulgar and common constitutions; but on such as are marked for virtue. He that can love his friend with this noble ardour will in a competent degree effect all. Now, if we can bring our affections to look beyond the body, and cast an eye upon the soul, we have found out the true object, not only of friendship, but charity: and the greatest happiness that we can bequeath the soul is that wherein we all do place our last felicity, salvation; which, though it be not in our power to bestow, it is in our charity and pious invocations to desire, if not procure and further. I cannot contentedly frame a prayer for myself in particular, without a catalogue for my friends; nor request a happiness wherein my sociable disposition doth not desire the fellowship of my neighbour. I never hear the toll of a passing bell, though in my mirth, without my prayers and best wishes for the departing spirit. I cannot go to cure the body of my patient, but I forget my profession, and call unto God for his soul. I cannot see one say his prayers, but, instead of imitating him, I fall into supplication for him, who perhaps is no more to me than a common nature: and if

God hath vouchsafed an ear to my supplications, there are surely many happy that never saw me, and enjoy the blessing of mine unknown devotions. To pray for enemies, that is, for their salvation, is no harsh precept, but the practice of our daily and ordinary devotions. I cannot believe the story of the Italian; our bad wishes and uncharitable desires proceed no further than this life; it is the devil, and the uncharitable votes of hell, that desire our misery in the world to come.

» (1642)

Of Silence

Margaret Cavendish Edited by John Pfannkuchen

1 It is said that silence is a great virtue: which is true in the chamber of a sick person who prefers quiet; or in the dead of night, or at lunchtimes when natural rest is not to be disturbed, or when superiors are nearby, or when someone else is speaking, or when attention should be given, or if the other person has great impediments of speech—in these cases speaking, many times, is dangerous, infamous, rude, foolish, malicious, envious, and false.

2 But it is a sad conversation that has no sound: and though silence is sometimes very commendable, in some cafes it is better to speak too much than too little; as in the case of hospitality when someone visits, because it's better that strangers and friends should think you talk too much than feel unwelcome by your speaking too little. Besides, it is a lesser fault to err on the side of too much courtesy, than with too much neglect. And being counted a fool is surely not so bad as as being counted rude: for the one is the fault of the judger, and the other is the fault of the actor or speaker, because civility is the life of society, and society is the life of human nature.

3 It is true, that there are more errors committed in speaking than in silence: because words are light and subtle, and too airy, that when they are once flown out they cannot be taken back, except by asking someone's pardon with more words: and there is an old saying: "To talk much, and well, is seldom heard". Which cannot be verified in all: for, some will speak well as long as there is grounds to speak on; but the length of time makes it sound to the ear as wine tastes to a drunken man, when he cannot relish between good and bad: so that it is not only the Matter, but the Manner, Time, and Subject, in Speaking, which makes it so hard to speak well, or please many: and though it be always pleasing to the Speaker to delight others; yet that doth not always please others, that he delights to speak of; as there is nothing more tedious to strangers, than to hear a man talk much of himself, or to weary them with long Complements; and though civility in that kind ought to be used; yet they should carry such forms and times, as not to lose respect to themselves, or to be over-troublesome in long expressions to others.

4   There are few but love to hear themselves talk; even Preachers: for a Preacher that preaches long, loves rather to talk than to edify the people; for the memory must not be oppressed in what they should learn; or their Reproofs too sharp in what they should mind; because if with one word or two of Reproof, he reforms; half a score undoes it again; which makes it a Railing instead of Exhortation. Neither is it required that a man should always speak according to his Profession or Employment in the Affairs of the world: for, it would be ridiculous for a Lawyer, in ordinary conversation, to speak as if he were pleading at the Bar; yet every one ought to have respect, in his Discourse, to his Condition; Calling, or Dignity, or to Quality of others: for it is not fit that there is a Priest, which either is or should be a Man of Peace, should speak like a Soldier, which is a Man of War; or speak to a Noble-man, as to a Priest.

5   Again, there is nothing take so much away the sweetness of Discourse, as long Preambles or Repetitions; and indeed, the whole Discourse is tedious and unpleasing, if it be over-long, though their Tongues were as smooth as Oil, and run upon the ways of truth; yet too much doth, as it were, over fill the Head, and stop the Ears: for, the Head will be as the Stomach, when it is over-charged, it will take surfeit of the most delicious Meat. Wherefore, in speaking, Judgement is required; yet some are so over-wise in the ordering of their Discourse, that it is not only troublesome to themselves, but a pain to the Hearers; having so set and constrained a way of speaking, as if their words went upon hard Scrues, when there is nothing so easy as Speech: for there is not part of man so unwearily active, as the Tongue. And of the other side, some are so full of talk,

that they will neither give room nor time to speak; and when two or three such persons, of this voluble quality or nature, meet, they make such a confusion in speaking all together, that it becomes a tumultuous noise, rather than a sociable discoursing; which is a disturbance to Society, because discourse should be like music in parts.

»   (1671)

A Piece of Chalk

G. K. Chesterton

1   I remember one splendid morning, all blue and silver, in the summer holidays when I reluctantly tore myself away from the task of doing nothing in particular, and put on a hat of some sort and picked up a walking-stick, and put six very bright-colored chalks in my pocket. I then went into the kitchen (which, along with the rest of the house, belonged to a very square and sensible old woman in a Sussex village), and asked the owner and occupant of the kitchen if she had any brown paper. She had a great deal; in fact, she had too much; and she mistook the purpose and the rationale of the existence of brown paper. She seemed to have an idea that if a person wanted brown paper he must be wanting to tie up parcels; which was the last thing I wanted to do; indeed, it is a thing which I have found to be beyond my mental capacity. Hence she dwelt very much on the varying qualities of toughness and endurance in the material. I explained to her that I only wanted to draw pictures on it, and that I did not want them to endure in the least; and that from my point of view, therefore, it was a question, not of tough consistency, but of responsive surface, a thing comparatively irrelevant in a parcel. When she understood that I wanted to draw she offered to overwhelm me with note-paper.

2   I then tried to explain the rather delicate logical shade, that I not only liked brown paper, but liked the quality of brownness in paper, just as I like the quality of brownness in October woods, or in beer. Brown paper represents the primal twilight of the first toil of creation, and with a bright-colored chalk or two you can pick out points of fire in it, sparks of gold, and blood-red, and sea-green, like the first fierce stars that sprang out of divine darkness. All this I said (in an off-hand way) to the old woman; and I put the brown paper in my pocket along with the chalks, and possibly other things. I suppose every one must have reflected how

primeval and how poetical are the things that one carries in one's pocket; the pocket-knife, for instance, the type of all human tools, the infant of the sword. Once I planned to write a book of poems entirely about things in my pockets. But I found it would be too long; and the age of the great epics is past. With my stick and my knife, my chalks and my brown paper, I went out on to the great downs…

3   I crossed one swell of living turf after another, looking for a place to sit down and draw. Do not, for heaven's sake, imagine I was going to sketch from Nature. I was going to draw devils and seraphim, and blind old gods that men worshipped before the dawn of right, and saints in robes of angry crimson, and seas of strange green, and all the sacred or monstrous symbols that look so well in bright colors on brown paper. They are much better worth drawing than Nature; also they are much easier to draw. When a cow came slouching by in the field next to me, a mere artist might have drawn it; but I always get wrong in the hind legs of quadrupeds. So I drew the soul of a cow; which I saw there plainly walking before me in the sunlight; and the soul was all purple and silver, and had seven horns and the mystery that belongs to all beasts. But though I could not with a crayon get the best out of the landscape, it does not follow that the landscape was not getting the best out of me. And this, I think, is the mistake that people make about the old poets who lived before Wordsworth, and were supposed not to care very much about Nature because they did not describe it much.

4   They preferred writing about great men to writing about great hills; but they sat on the great hills to write it. They gave out much less about Nature, but they drank in, perhaps, much more. They painted the white robes of their holy virgins with the blinding snow, at which they had stared all day…The greenness of a thousand green leaves clustered into the live green figure of Robin Hood. The blueness of a score of forgotten skies became the blue robes of the Virgin. The inspiration went in like sunbeams and came out

like Apollo.

5　But as I sat scrawling these silly figures on the brown paper, it began to dawn on me, to my great disgust, that I had left one chalk, and that a most exquisite and essential chalk, behind. I searched all my pockets, but I could not find any white chalk. Now, those who are acquainted with all the philosophy (nay, religion) which is typified in the art of drawing on brown paper, know that white is positive and essential. I cannot avoid remarking here upon a moral significance. One of the wise and awful truths which this brown-paper art reveals, is this, that white is a color. It is not a mere absence of color; it is a shining and affirmative thing, as fierce as red, as definite as black. When, so to speak, your pencil grows red-hot, it draws roses; when it grows white-hot, it draws stars. And one of the two or three defiant verities of the best religious morality, of real Christianity, for example, is exactly this same thing; the chief assertion of religious morality is that white is a color. Virtue is not the absence of vices or the avoidance of moral dangers; virtue is a vivid and separate thing, like pain or a particular smell. Mercy does not mean not being cruel, or sparing people revenge or punishment; it means a plain and positive thing like the sun, which one has either seen or not seen.

6　Chastity does not mean abstention from sexual wrong; it means something flaming, like Joan of Arc. In a word, God paints in many colors; but he never paints so gorgeously, I had almost said so gaudily, as when He paints in white. In a sense our age has realized this fact, and expressed it in our sullen costume. For if it were really true that white was a blank and colorless thing, negative and non-committal, then white would be used instead of black and gray for the funereal dress of this pessimistic period. Which is not the case.

7　Meanwhile I could not find my chalk.

8　I sat on the hill in a sort of despair. There was no town near at which it was even remotely probable there would be such a thing as an artist's colorant. And yet, without any white, my absurd little pictures would be as pointless as the world would be if there were no good people in it. I stared stupidly round, racking my brain for expedients. Then I suddenly stood up and roared with laughter, again and again, so that the cows stared at me and called a committee. Imagine a man in the Sahara regretting that he had no sand for his hour-glass. Imagine a gentleman in mid-ocean wishing that he had brought some salt water with him for his chemical experiments. I was sitting on an immense warehouse of white chalk. The landscape was made entirely of white chalk. White chalk was piled more miles until it met the sky. I stooped and broke a piece of the rock I sat on: it did not mark so well as the shop chalks do, but it gave the effect. And I stood there in a trance of pleasure, realizing that this Southern England is not only a grand peninsula, and a tradition and a civilization; it is something even more admirable. It is a piece of chalk.

»   (1905)

On Running After One's Hat

G. K. Chesterton

1   I feel an almost savage envy on hearing that London has been flooded in my absence, while I am in the mere country. My own Battersea has been, I understand, particularly favoured as a meeting of the waters. Battersea was already, as I need hardly say, the most beautiful of human localities. Now that it has the additional splendour of great sheets of water, there must be something quite incomparable in the landscape (or waterscape) of my own romantic town. Battersea must be a vision of Venice. The boat that brought the meat from the butcher's must have shot along those lanes of rippling silver with the strange smoothness of the gondola. The greengrocer who brought cabbages to the corner of the Latchmere Road must have leant upon the oar with the unearthly grace of the gondolier. There is nothing so perfectly poetical as an island; and when a district is flooded it becomes an archipelago.

2   Some consider such romantic views of flood or fire slightly lacking in reality. But really this romantic view of such inconveniences is quite as practical as the other. The true optimist who sees in such things an opportunity for enjoyment is quite as logical and much more sensible than the ordinary "Indignant Ratepayer" who sees in them an opportunity for grumbling. Real pain, as in the case of being burnt at Smithfield or having a toothache, is a positive thing; it can be supported, but scarcely enjoyed. But, after all, our toothaches are the exception, and as for being burnt at Smithfield, it only happens to us at the very longest intervals. And most of the inconveniences that make men swear or women cry are really sentimental or imaginative inconveniences—things altogether of the mind. For instance, we often hear grown-up people complaining of having to hang about a railway station and wait for a train. Did you ever hear a small boy complain of having to hang about a railway station and wait for a train? No; for to him to be inside a railway

station is to be inside a cavern of wonder and a palace of poetical pleasures. Because to him the red light and the green light on the signal are like a new sun and a new moon. Because to him when the wooden arm of the signal falls down suddenly, it is as if a great king had thrown down his staff as a signal and started a shrieking tournament of trains. I myself am of little boys' habit in this matter. They also serve who only stand and wait for the two fifteen. Their meditations may be full of rich and fruitful things. Many of the most purple hours of my life have been passed at Clapham Junction, which is now, I suppose, under water. I have been there in many moods so fixed and mystical that the water might well have come up to my waist before I noticed it particularly. But in the case of all such annoyances, as I have said, everything depends upon the emotional point of view. You can safely apply the test to almost every one of the things that are currently talked of as the typical nuisance of daily life.

3   For instance, there is a current impression that it is unpleasant to have to run after one's hat. Why should it be unpleasant to the well-ordered and pious mind? Not merely because it is running, and running exhausts one. The same people run much faster in games and sports. The same people run much more eagerly after an uninteresting, little leather ball than they will after a nice silk hat. There is an idea that it is humiliating to run after one's hat; and when people say it is humiliating they mean that it is comic. It certainly is comic; but man is a very comic creature, and most of the things he does are comic—eating, for instance. And the most comic things of all are exactly the things that are most worth doing—such as making love. A man running after a hat is not half so ridiculous as a man running after a wife.

4   Now a man could, if he felt rightly in the matter, run after his hat with the manliest ardour and the most sacred joy. He might regard himself as a jolly huntsman pursuing a wild animal, for certainly no animal could be wilder. In fact, I am inclined to believe that

hat-hunting on windy days will be the sport of the upper classes in the future. There will be a meet of ladies and gentlemen on some high ground on a gusty morning. They will be told that the professional attendants have started a hat in such-and-such a thicket, or whatever be the technical term. Notice that this employment will in the fullest degree combine sport with humanitarianism. The hunters would feel that they were not inflicting pain. Nay, they would feel that they were inflicting pleasure, rich, almost riotous pleasure, upon the people who were looking on. When last I saw an old gentleman running after his hat in Hyde Park, I told him that a heart so benevolent as his ought to be filled with peace and thanks at the thought of how much unaffected pleasure his every gesture and bodily attitude were at that moment giving to the crowd.

5   The same principle can be applied to every other typical domestic worry. A gentleman trying to get a fly out of the milk or a piece of cork out of his glass of wine often imagines himself to be irritated. Let him think for a moment of the patience of anglers sitting by dark pools, and let his soul be immediately irradiated with gratification and repose. Again, I have known some people of very modern views driven by their distress to the use of theological terms to which they attached no doctrinal significance, merely because a drawer was jammed tight and they could not pull it out. A friend of mine was particularly afflicted in this way. Every day his drawer was jammed, and every day in consequence it was something else that rhymes to it. But I pointed out to him that this sense of wrong was really subjective and relative; it rested entirely upon the assumption that the drawer could, should, and would come out easily. "But if," I said, "you picture to yourself that you are pulling against some powerful and oppressive enemy, the struggle will become merely exciting and not exasperating. Imagine that you are tugging up a lifeboat out of the sea. Imagine that you are roping up a fellow-creature out of an Alpine crevass. Imagine even that you are a boy again and engaged in a tug-of-war between French and

English." Shortly after saying this I left him; but I have no doubt at all that my words bore the best possible fruit. I have no doubt that every day of his life he hangs on to the handle of that drawer with a flushed face and eyes bright with battle, uttering encouraging shouts to himself, and seeming to hear all round him the roar of an applauding ring.

6 So I do not think that it is altogether fanciful or incredible to suppose that even the floods in London may be accepted and enjoyed poetically. Nothing beyond inconvenience seems really to have been caused by them; and inconvenience, as I have said, is only one aspect, and that the most unimaginative and accidental aspect of a really romantic situation. An adventure is only an inconvenience rightly considered. An inconvenience is only an adventure wrongly considered. The water that girdled the houses and shops of London must, if anything, have only increased their previous witchery and wonder. For as the Roman Catholic priest in the story said: "Wine is good with everything except water," and on a similar principle, water is good with everything except wine.

»   (1908)

On Lying in Bed

G. K. Chesterton

1 Lying in bed would be an altogether perfect and supreme experience if only one had a coloured pencil long enough to draw on the ceiling. This, however, is not generally a part of the domestic apparatus on the premises. I think myself that the thing might be managed with several pails of Aspinall and a broom. Only if one worked in a really sweeping and masterly way, and laid on the colour in great washes, it might drip down again on one's face in floods of rich and mingled colour like some strange fairy rain; and that would have its disadvantages. I am afraid it would be necessary to stick to black and white in this form of artistic composition. To that purpose, indeed, the white ceiling would be of the greatest possible use; in fact, it is the only use I think of a white ceiling being put to.

2 But for the beautiful experiment of lying in bed I might never have discovered it. For years I have been looking for some blank spaces in a modern house to draw on. Paper is much too small for any really allegorical design; as Cyrano de Bergerac says, "Il me faut des géants" ["I need giants"]. But when I tried to find these fine clear spaces in the modern rooms such as we all live in I was continually disappointed. I found an endless pattern and complication of small objects hung like a curtain of fine links between me and my desire. I examined the walls; I found them to my surprise to be already covered with wallpaper, and I found the wallpaper to be already covered with uninteresting images, all bearing a ridiculous resemblance to each other. I could not understand why one arbitrary symbol (a symbol apparently entirely devoid of any religious or philosophical significance) should thus be sprinkled all over my nice walls like a sort of small-pox. The Bible must be referring to wallpapers, I think, when it says, "Use not vain repetitions, as the Gentiles do." I found the Turkey carpet a mass of unmeaning

colours, rather like the Turkish Empire, or like the sweetmeat called Turkish Delight. I do not exactly know what Turkish Delight really is; but I suppose it is Macedonian Massacres. Everywhere that I went forlornly, with my pencil or my paint brush, I found that others had unaccountably been before me, spoiling the walls, the curtains, and the furniture with their childish and barbaric designs.

. . . . .

3 Nowhere did I find a really clear space for sketching until this occasion when I prolonged beyond the proper limit the process of lying on my back in bed. Then the light of that white heaven broke upon my vision, that breadth of mere white which is indeed almost the definition of Paradise, since it means purity and also means freedom. But alas! like all heavens, now that it is seen it is found to be unattainable; it looks more austere and more distant than the blue sky outside the window. For my proposal to paint on it with the bristly end of a broom has been discouraged—never mind by whom; by a person debarred from all political rights—and even my minor proposal to put the other end of the broom into the kitchen fire and turn it to charcoal has not been conceded. Yet I am certain that it was from persons in my position that all the original inspiration came for covering the ceilings of palaces and cathedrals with a riot of fallen angels or victorious gods. I am sure that it was only because Michael Angelo was engaged in the ancient and honourable occupation of lying in bed that he ever realized how the roof of the Sistine Chapel might be made into an awful imitation of a divine drama that could only be acted in the heavens.

4 The tone now commonly taken toward the practice of lying in bed is hypocritical and unhealthy. Of all the marks of modernity that seem to mean a kind of decadence, there is none more menacing and dangerous than the exultation of very small and secondary matters of conduct at the expense of very great and primary ones, at the expense of eternal ties and tragic human morality. If there is one thing worse than the modern weakening of major morals, it is

the modern strengthening of minor morals. Thus it is considered more withering to accuse a man of bad taste than of bad ethics. Cleanliness is not next to godliness nowadays, for cleanliness is made essential and godliness is regarded as an offence. A playwright can attack the institution of marriage so long as he does not misrepresent the manners of society, and I have met Ibsenite pessimists who thought it wrong to take beer but right to take prussic acid. Especially this is so in matters of hygiene; notably such matters as lying in bed. Instead of being regarded, as it ought to be, as a matter of personal convenience and adjustment, it has come to be regarded by many as if it were a part of essential morals to get up early in the morning. It is upon the whole part of practical wisdom; but there is nothing good about it or bad about its opposite. . . . . .

5 Misers get up early in the morning; and burglars, I am informed, get up the night before. It is the great peril of our society that all its mechanisms may grow more fixed while its spirit grows more fickle. A man's minor actions and arrangements ought to be free, flexible, creative; the things that should be unchangeable are his principles, his ideals. But with us the reverse is true; our views change constantly; but our lunch does not change. Now, I should like men to have strong and rooted conceptions, but as for their lunch, let them have it sometimes in the garden, sometimes in bed, sometimes on the roof, sometimes in the top of a tree. Let them argue from the same first principles, but let them do it in a bed, or a boat, or a balloon. This alarming growth of good habits really means a too great emphasis on those virtues which mere custom can ensure, it means too little emphasis on those virtues which custom can never quite ensure, sudden and splendid virtues of inspired pity or of inspired candour. If ever that abrupt appeal is made to us we may fail. A man can get used to getting up at five o'clock in the morning. A man cannot very well get used to being burnt for his opinions; the first experiment is commonly fatal. Let us pay a little more attention to these possibilities of the heroic and

unexpected. I dare say that when I get out of this bed I shall do some deed of an almost terrible virtue.

6   For those who study the great art of lying in bed there is one emphatic caution to be added. Even for those who can do their work in bed (like journalists), still more for those whose work cannot be done in bed (as, for example, the professional harpooners of whales), it is obvious that the indulgence must be very occasional. But that is not the caution I mean. The caution is this: if you do lie in bed, be sure you do it without any reason or justification at all. I do not speak, of course, of the seriously sick. But if a healthy man lies in bed, let him do it without a rag of excuse; then he will get up a healthy man. If he does it for some secondary hygienic reason, if he has some scientific explanation, he may get up a hypochondriac.

»   (1909)

Loss of Speech Through Isolation

Anna Julia Cooper

1 One summer during the World War as War Camp Community Service I had charge of a playground in West Virginia.

2 Standing out conspicuously in my impressions of that summer's experiences is a family whom I shall call Berry—chiefly because that is not their name. The two lads, about ten and twelve, who first presented themselves to my acquaintanceship were perfect little Ishmaelites—their hand against everybody and every man's hand against them. Teachers of the neighborhood said that their school record was simply an annual repetition of suspensions and expulsions. They would present themselves regularly in September all spic and span with clean shirts, clean, if patched trousers, and clean eager faces for the year's start; but something always happened before the first lap of the course was run, and everybody thought the Berry boys lucky if October found them still on "praying ground where e'en the vilest sinner may return."

3 They were rather shy of the playground, especially when other children were there having a good time. Decidedly anti-social, they would slip in after the gates were shut and the swings locked, pick or break the locks to enjoy criminally what they might have had freely by simply being in the current with other people. They were never openly and bravely bad—they were only bad as rats are bad—with a passion and a genius for getting around all constituted authority. They would delight in climbing a hill overlooking the playground whence they would roll down boulders and huge stones that came crashing to a full stop just outside the limits of my jurisdiction. I noticed that their bedevilment was peculiarly voiceless. Most urchins of that type would be ready to sing out in fiendish glee when they thought they had you wrought up to a charming pitch of impotent rage. Not so the Berry boys. In fact

they resembled nothing more than the silent little old men of the mountains that Rip saw amusing themselves at ninepins; and if you uttered the word "police!" the whole panorama would disappear so quickly, vanishing so completely you would imagine it had all been a horrid nightmare, and there wasn't any such thing as Berry boys after all—You had been dreaming!

4   One day when I was almost alone on the playground in consequence of a steady drizzle all forenoon, I noticed a forlorn little figure with a pair of big round mellow eyes, peeping at me through chinks in the palings. As I started down to speak to her, the frightened little creature, a child of five or six made a dash as tho she would run away. I coaxed her in and putting her in one of the little folks' swings, stood by giving her a gentle push now and then, an excitement that she enjoyed very much. Tho she said nothing, one could read her gratitude in those lustrous round eyes—her joy was too deep for utterance. Alas, short lived joy! A tall soldier lad in khaki, puttees and an over-seas cap, came stalking up the walk. Without recognizing me or uttering a word he took a position at the rear where he caught the eye of the little mite in the swing. The effect was electrical. The child fell out of the swing as if she had been shot! And pit-a-pat, pit-a-pat, as fast as her little legs could carry her she flew, neither looking back nor waving goodbye. Startled out of my Olympian calm, I turned on the strange and demanded to know what was the matter.

5   "Meh wants her hom," he replied sententiously.

6   "Yes? but why didn't you say your mother and father sent for her? You haven't said a word!"

7   "She know what I mean."

8   "Perhaps! But it isn't right for you to deal in dumb signs in conveying what you mean. You owe that child the English language. You are grown and have traveled. You can express yourself and interest her in the wonderful world outside that you have had glimpses of.

She will never be anything but a dumb, shut-in creature unless you make opportunities for her to cultivate human speech!" More of the same sort I poured forth out of a full heart from my accustomed store. What struck me all the time I was talking was the unbroken stolidity with which my bursts of eloquence were received. He showed neither resentment at the lambasting I gave him nor a gleam of appreciation that was fairly well done for a woman. He was chewing a bit of wheat straw pulled in the field and regarded me with the patient, passionless eyes of a yoke of oxen at the end of a furrow when the day is done. Finally in sheer desperation at getting no response, I turned on my heel and left him. Reaching down he pulled another bit of straw which he caught in his teeth and stalked out as he had stalked in. My notebook records this day: "Encounter with the oldest and youngest of the Berry family."

9   Act II, Scene 1, discovers me in the midst of my basket weavers, reed and raffia all around and busy little fingers holding up mats and baskets in various stages of imperfection—all clamoring to be set right and shown how at the same instant. Walter Berry, the younger of the two tormentors I had known from the first on the playground, now becoming less shy and perhaps, too, a little less savage, was hovering near the background, evidently struggling with something he wanted to say but having a hard time getting it out. At last he sidled up, and speaking over my shoulder from behind me managed to blurt out desperately:

10 "Mith Coo' show—I make bick too!"

11 "Why certainly, Walter, " I said with ready comprehension. "I'll be glad to show you how to make a bas-ket," speaking very distinctly and letting him observe the motion of my lips in pronouncing "bas-ket." "You must try to come every day and you have to take lots of pains, you know. But it will be real nice to make a basket for your mother.—Don't you think so?"

12 Well, from that day till the end of my stay I was taming Walter and incidentally getting a basket ready to present to his mother.

Not infrequently I had to take out at night what Walter had put in by day so as to have him start right the next day, but on the whole the basket, between us, got on amazingly well and I determined to use it as a card of introduction to Mrs. Berry the "Meh" of whom I had heard much but never seen. Accordingly, armed with my playground products I fared forth to break the ice and force a passage into some homes I had never succeeded in luring out to any of our many tempting "occasions" at the playground.

13 Mrs. Berry's was my first coup de main. The house was at the top of a high hill with more steps to climb to reach the porch which spanned a plain but scrupulously neat living room. The floor was freshly scrubbed with white sand, there was a deal table also scrubbed to snowy whiteness and a few splint bottomed chairs scrubbed likewise. All this I noticed standing on the threshold of the front door which stood wide open from habit, one could see, rather than with any notion of inviting wayfarers to enter. I knocked on the floor with the point of my umbrella and after some minutes a comely little black woman appeared in the doorway just opposite and stood with hands crossed in front of her waiting to learn the cause of the intrusion.

14 "Oh," I said with an ingratiating smile; "This is Mrs. Berry, is it not? I am Mrs. Cooper, Walter's teacher on the playground. I came to bring you a little basket that Walter made for you—I taught him how," I added truthfully. "Rather pretty don't you think?" Appealingly now—for I was becoming a wee bit fazed a whipping my own top. For the lady held her pose of dignified aloofness in queenly silence. She might have been an artist's conception of Juno just after that goatherd Paris had pinned the blue ribbon on his amorous little charmer. She did not frown, neither did she beam a smile. She did not ask me in nor say that she was glad I brought the basket. She did not make a pretence of thanking me for any interest I had taken in Walter nor did she try to act out the lie that she was glad to meet me, and yet with it all her manner was singularly free

from active repulsion. Bryon's line comes to mind: "I seek to shun, not hate mankind," and yet Bryon's misanthropy was a pose put on to write about it, and the curl of his patrician lip, the négligé of his open collar and the somber lilt of his dreamy eyes were sedulously cultivated before the mirror by all the dudes and dandies in New York and London. But here in this solitary little woman was something that was no pose, something, I felt instinctively, too sacred for prying eyes and inquisitive "investigators." She stood and appraised me with that same unfrowning eye I had noticed in her first born that made you think of uncomplaining oxen, too strong to weep, too weighted down to smile.

15 After a while she parted her lips—and this is what she said: "I keep to myself; I don' want nothin' to do wit nobody." Her tone was even and clear without the slightest suspicion of hysteria or overwrought emotion. The words might have been borne in from a disembodied spirit, so passionless were they, so sublimated, so purified of the tenseness and dross of the physical and earthly.

16 "But Mrs. Berry, " I persisted, "You can't live that way! You can't be in the world without having something to do with other people!"

17 "I been living' that way longer'n you been livin' yo' way," she rejoined, "I'm older'n you." (She wasn't at all; but a comparatively young woman.) I accepted the compliment without debate, however, and tried by the most beguiling arts I knew to entice her out of her solitude. After using all the illustrations and arguments I could think of to suggest the interdependence of man on man I was rewarded by seeing the merest ghost of a smile flit across her countenance, more like the quivering gleam of faraway lightning than the steady radiance of sunlight and dawn. We were still standing where I could look out from the threshold of the porch on the muddy water of the Ohio River. "There's nothing you could get to eat," I continued, "without calling in someone to help you out. You can go to the river and fish—"

18 "And then I'd have to have lard to cook 'em wit," she put in brightly.

19 Good! I knew I had struck fire and we were friends at last.

20 As I came down the steps she called out almost shamefastly, "When you come to W—again, come to see me!"

21 "Oh, no," I bantered—"you don't want to see anybody!"

22 "Well, if all was like you," she answered dismally.

23 It was not till I had left W—that I understood the tragedy of Mrs. Berry's grim struggle with life. Her husband, an innocent man, had been torn from her arms by an infuriated mob and brutally murdered—lynched. The town realized its mistake afterwards when the true culprit confessed but it was too late to bind up that broken family, and the humble drama of that obscure black woman like a wounded animal with her cubs literally digging herself in and then at bay dumbly turning to face—America—her "head bloody but unbowed"—I swear the pathos and inexorable fatefulness of that titanic struggle—an inescapable one in the clash of American forces, is worthy an Epic for its heroic grandeur and unconquerable grit!

24 And I wondered what our brand of education, what our smug injunction that the home "is expected" to cooperate with the school will find or from American environmental conditions as are the blind fish in the Mamoth Cave or the broncos of the western plains.

25 A Problem—Will isolation solve it?

» (1923)

Murder as a Fine Art

Thomas De Quincy Edited by John Pfannkuchen

1   A new paper on Murder as a Fine Art might open thus: that on the model of those Gentlemen Radicals who had voted a monument to Palmer, etc., it was proposed to erect statues to such murderers as by their next-of-kin, or other person interested in their glory. Such persons should make out a claim either of superior atrocity, or, in equal atrocity, of superior neatness, continuity of execution, perfect preparation or felicitous originality, smoothness or curiosa felicitas (elaborate felicity).

2   The men who murdered the cat, as we read in the Newgate Calendar, were good, but Williams better who murdered the baby. And perhaps (but the hellish felicity of the last act makes us demur) Fielding was superior. For you never hear of a fire swallowing up a fire, or a rain stopping a deluge (for this would be a reign of Kilkenny cats); but what fire, deluge, or Kilkenny cats could not do, Fielding proposed, viz., to murder the murderers, to become himself the Nemesis. Fielding was the murderer of murderers in a double sense—rhetorical and literal. But that was, after all, a small matter compared with the fine art of the man calling himself Outis, on which for a moment we must dwell. Outis—so at all events he was called, but doubtless he indulged in many aliases—at Nottingham joined vehemently and sincerely, as it seemed, in pursuit of a wretch taxed with having murdered, twelve years previously, a wife and two children at Halifax, which wretch (when all the depositions were before the magistrate) turned out to be the aforesaid Mr. Outis. That suggests a wide field of speculation and reference.

3   Note the power of murderers as fine-art professors to make a new start, to turn the corner, to retreat upon the road they have come, as though it were new to them, and to make diversions that disarm suspicion. This they owe to fortunate obscurity, which attests

anew the wonderful compensations of life; for celebrity and power combine to produce drawbacks.

4   A foreigner who lands in Calcutta at an hour which nobody can name, and endeavours to effect a sneaking entrance at the postern-gate of the governor-general's palace, may be a decent man; but this we know, that he has cut the towing-rope which bound his own boat to the great ark of his country. It may be that, in leaving Paris or Naples, he was simply cutting the connection with creditors who showed signs of attachment not good for his health. But it may also be that he ran away by the blaze of a burning inn, which he had fired in order to hide three throats which he had cut, and nine purses which he had stolen. There is no guarantee for such a man's character.

5   Have we, then, no such rascals at home? No, not in the classes standing favorably for promotion. The privilege of safe criminality, not liable to exposure, is limited to classes crowded together like leaves in Vallombrosa; for them to run away into some mighty city, Manchester or Glasgow, is to commence life anew. They turn over a new leaf with a vengeance. Many are the carpenters, bricklayers, bakers' apprentices, etc., who are now living decently in Bristol, Newcastle, Hull, Liverpool, after marrying sixteen wives, and leaving families to the care of twelve separate parishes.

6   That scamp is at this moment circulating and gyrating in society, like a respectable totum, though we don't know his exact name, who, if he were pleased to reveal himself in seventeen parts of this kingdom, where (to use the police language) he has been 'wanted' for some years, would be hanged seventeen times running, besides putting seventeen Government rewards into the pockets of seventeen policemen.

7   Oh, reader, you little know the unutterable romances perpetrated for ever in our most populous empire, under cloud of night and distance and utter poverty, Mark that—of utter poverty. Wealth is power; but it is a jest in comparison of poverty. Splendour is

power; but it is a joke to obscurity. To be poor, to be obscure, to be a baker's apprentice or a tailor's journeyman, throws a power about a man, clothes him with attributes of ubiquity, really with those privileges of concealment which in the ring of Gyges were but fabulous. Is it a king, is it a sultan, that such a man rivals? Oh, friend, he rivals a spiritual power.

8   Two men are on record, perhaps many more might have been on that record, who wrote so many books, and perpetrated so many pamphlets, that at fifty they had forgotten much of their own literary villainies, and at sixty they commenced with murderous ferocity a series of answers to arguments which it was proved upon them afterwards that they themselves had emitted at thirty—thus coming round with volleys of small shot on their own heads, as the Whispering Gallery at St. Paul's begins to retaliate any secrets you have committed to its keeping in echoing thunders after a time, or as Sir John Mandeville under Arctic skies heard in May all those curses thawing, and exploding like minute-guns, which had been frozen up in November. Even like those self-replying authors, even like those self-reverberators in St. Paul's, even like those Arctic practitioners in cursing, who drew bills and post obits in malediction, which were to be honoured after the death of winter, many men are living at this moment in merry England who have figured in so many characters, illustrated so many villages, run away from so many towns, and performed the central part in so many careers, that were the character, the village, the town, the career, brought back with all its circumstances to their memories, positively they would fail to recognise their own presence or incarnation in their own acts and bodies.

9   We have all read the story told by Addison of a sultan, who was persuaded by a dervish to dip his head into a basin of enchanted water, and thereupon found himself upon some other globe, a son in a poor man's family, married after certain years the woman of his heart, had a family of seven children whom he painfully brought

up, went afterwards through many persecutions, walked pensively by the seashore meditating some escape from his miseries, bathed in the sea as a relief from the noon-day heat, and on lifting up his head from the waves found himself lifting up his head from the basin into which that cursed dervish had persuaded him to dip. And when he would have cudgelled the holy man for that long life of misery which had, through his means, been inflicted upon himself, behold! the holy man proved by affidavit that, in this world, at any rate (where only he could be punishable), the life had lasted but thirty-three seconds.

10 Even so do the dark careers of many amongst our obscure and migratory villains from years shrink up to momentary specks, or, by their very multitude, altogether evanesce. Burke and Hare, it is well known, had lost all count of their several murders; they no more remembered, or could attempt to remember, their separate victims, than a respectable old banker of seventy-three can remember all the bills with their indorsements made payable for half-a-century at his bank; or than Foote's turnpike-keeper, who had kept all the toll-bar tickets to Kensington for forty-eight years, pretended to recollect the features of all the men who had delivered them at his gate. For a time, perhaps, Burke (who was a man of fine sensibility) had a representative vision of spasms, and struggles, and convulsions, terminating in a ten-pound note indorsed by Dr. Someone. Hare, on the other hand, was a man of principle, a man that you could depend upon—order a corpse for Friday, and on Friday you had it—but he had no feeling whatsoever. Yet see the unity of result for him and Burke. For both alike all troublesome recollections gathered into one blue haze of heavenly abstractions: orders executed with fidelity, cheques on the bankers to be crossed and passed and cashed, are no more remembered. That is the acme of perfection in our art.

11 One great class of criminals I am aware of in past times as having specially tormented myself—the class who have left secrets, riddles,

behind them. What business has any man to bequeath a conundrum to all posterity, unless he leaves in some separate channel the solution? This must have been done in malice, and for the purpose of annoying us, lest we should have too much proper enjoyment of life when he should have gone. For nobody knows whether the scoundrel could have solved it himself—too like in that respect to some charades which, in my boyish days (but then I had the excuse of youth, which they had not), I not unfrequently propounded to young ladies. Take this as a specimen: My first raises a little hope; my second very little indeed; and my whole is a vast roar of despair. No young lady could ever solve it; neither could I. We all had to give it up. A charade that only needs an answer, which, perhaps, some distant generation may supply, is but a half and half, tentative approach to this. Very much of this nature was the genius or Daimon (don't say Demon) of Socrates. How many thousands of learned writers and printers have gone to sleep over too profound attempts to solve that, which Socrates ought to have been able to solve at sight. I am myself of opinion that it was a dram-bottle, which someone raised a ghost to explain.

12 Then the Entelecheia of Aristotle; did you ever read about that, excellent reader? Most people fancy it to have meant some unutterable crotchet in metaphysics, some horrible idea (lest the police should be after it) without a name; that is, until the Stagyrite repaired the injustice of his conduct by giving it a pretty long one. My opinion now, as you are anxious to know it, is, that it was a lady, a sweetheart of Aristotle's; for what was to hinder Aristotle having a sweetheart?

13 I dare say Thomas Aquinas, dry and arid as he was, raised his unprincipled eyes to some Neapolitan beauty, began a sonnet to some lady's eyebrow, though he might forget to finish it. And my belief is that this lady, ambitious as Semele, wished to be introduced as an eternal jewel into the great vault of her lover's immortal Philosophy, which was to travel much farther and agitate far longer

than his royal pupil's conquests. Upon that Aristotle, keeping her hand, said: 'My love, I'll think of it.' And then it occurred to him, that in the very heavens many lovely ladies, Andromeda, Cassiopeia, Ariadne, etc., had been placed as constellations in that map which many chronologists suppose to have been prepared for the use of the ship Argo, a whole generation before the Trojan war. Berenice, though he could not be aware of that, had interest even to procure a place in that map for her ringlets; and of course for herself she might have. Considering which, Aristotle said: 'Hang me! if I don't put her among the ten Categories!' On after thoughts he put her higher, for an Entelecheia is as much above a Category as our Padishah Victoria is above a Turkish sultan. 'But now, Stag,' said the lady (privileged as a sweetheart she called him Stag, though everybody else was obliged to call him Stagyrite), 'how will they know it's meant for me, Stag?' Upon which I am sorry to say the philosopher fell to cursing and swearing, bestowing blessings on his own optics and on posterity's, meaning yours and mine, saying: 'Let them find it out.' Well, now, you see I have found it out. But that is more than I hope for my crypto-criminals, and therefore I take this my only way of giving them celebration and malediction in one breath.

FOOTNOTES:

14 Notwithstanding what he had written in the essay on the 'Essenes,' no doubt De Quincey, if he had completed this paper, could not have escaped characteristic, and perhaps grimly humorous, references of his own to the Sicarii, of whom Josephus has a good deal to tell in his 'Jewish War'; for it seems to us his thoughts were bearing directly that way. Josephus says of the Sicarii: 'In these days there arose another sort of robbers in Jerusalem, who were named Sicarii, who slew men in the day-time and in the middle of the city, more especially at the festivals. There they mixed with the multitude, and having concealed little daggers under their garments,

with these they stabbed those that were their enemies; and when any fell down dead, the murderers joined the bystanders in expressing their indignation; so that from their plausibilities they could by no means be discovered. The first man that was slain by them was Jonathan the high-priest, after which many were slain every day.'—Ed.

15 'Postern-gate.' See the legend of Sir Eustace the Crusader, and the good Sir Hubert, who 'sounded the horn which he alone could sound,' as told by Wordsworth.

» (1827)

The Almost Perfect State

Don Marquis

I

1   No matter how nearly perfect an Almost Perfect State may be, it is not nearly enough perfect unless the individuals who compose it can, somewhere between death and birth, have a perfectly corking time for a few years. The most wonderful governmental system in the world does not attract us, as a system; we are after a system that scarcely knows it is a system; the great thing is to have the largest number of individuals as happy as may be, for a little while at least, some time before they die.

2   Infancy is not what it is cracked up to be. The child seems happy all the time to the adult, because the adult knows that the child is untouched by the real problems of life; if the adult were similarly untouched he is sure that he would be happy. But children, not knowing that they are having an easy time, have a good many hard times. Growing and learning and obeying the rules of their elders, of fighting against them, are not easy things to do. Adolescence is certainly far from a uniformly pleasant period. Early manhood might be the most glorious time of all were it not that the sheer excess of life and vigor gets a fellow into continual scrapes. Of middle age the best that can be said is that a middle aged person has likely learned how to have a little fun in spite of his troubles.

3   It is to old age that we look for reimbursement, the most of us. And most of us look in vain. For the most of us have been wrenched and racked, in one way or another, until old age is the most trying time of all.

4   In the Almost Perfect State every person shall have at least ten years before he dies of easy, carefree, happy living...things will be so

arranged economically that this will be possible for each individual.

5 Personally we look forward to an old age of dissipation and indolence and unreverend disrepute. In fifty years we shall be ninety-two years old. We intend to work rather hard during those fifty years and accumulate enough to live on without working any more for the next ten years, for we have determined to die at the age of one hundred two.

6 During the last ten years we shall indulge ourself in many things that we have been forced by circumstances to forego. We have always been compelled, and we shall be compelled for many years to come, to be prudent, cautious, staid, sober, conservative, industrious, respectful of established institutions, a model citizen. We have not liked it, but we have been unable to escape it. Our mind, our logical faculties, our observation, inform us that the conservatives have the right side of the argument in all human affairs. But the people whom we really prefer as associates, though we do not approve their ideas, are the rebels, the radicals, the wastrels, the vicious, the poets, the Bolshevists, the idealists, the nuts, the Lucifers, the agreeable good-for-nothings, the sentimentalists, the prophets, the freaks. We have never dared to know any of them, far less become intimate with them.

7 Between the years of ninety-two and a hundred and two, however, we shall be the ribald, useless, drunken outcast person we have always wished to be. We shall have a long white beard and long white hair; we shall not walk at all, but recline in a wheel chair and bellow for alcoholic beverages; in the winter we shall sit before the fire with our feet in a bucket of hot water, with a decanter of corn whiskey near at hand, and write ribald songs against organized society; strapped to one arm of our chair will be a forty-five caliber revolver, and we shall shoot out the lights when we want to go to sleep, instead of turning them off; when we want air we shall throw a silver candlestick through the front window and be damned to it; we shall address public meetings to which we have

been invited because of our wisdom in a vein of jocund malice. We shall...but we don't wish to make any one envious of the good time that is coming to us...we look forward to a disreputable, vigorous, unhonored and disorderly old age.

8 (In the meantime, of course, you understand you can't have us pinched and deported for our yearnings.)

9 We shall know that the Almost Perfect State is here when the kind of old age each person wants is possible to him. Of course, all of you may not want the kind we want...some of you may prefer prunes and morality to the bitter end. Some of you may be dissolute now and may look forward to becoming like one of the nice old fellows in a Wordsworth poem. But for our part we have always been a hypocrite and we shall have to continue being a hypocrite for a good many years yet, and we yearn to come out in our true colors at last. The point is, that no matter what you want to be, during those last ten years, that you may be, in the Almost Perfect State.

10 Any system of government under which the individual does all the sacrificing for the sake of the general good, for the sake of the community, the State, gets off on its wrong foot. We don't want things that cost us too much. We don't want too much strain all the time.

11 The best good that you can possibly achieve is not good enough if you have to strain yourself all the time to reach it. A thing is only worth doing, and doing again and again, if you can do it rather easily, and get some joy out of it.

12 Do the best you can, without straining yourself too much and too continuously, and leave the rest to God. If you strain yourself too much you'll have to ask God to patch you up. And for all you know, patching you up may take time that it was planned to use some other way.

13 BUT...overstrain yourself now and then. For this reason: The

things you create easily and joyously will not continue to come easily and joyously unless you yourself are getting bigger all the time. And when you overstrain yourself you are assisting in the creation of a new self—if you get what we mean. And if you should ask us suddenly just what this has to do with the picture of the old guy in the wheel chair we should answer: Hanged if we know, but we seemed to sort o' run into it, somehow.

II

14 Interplanetary communication is one of the persistent dreams of the inhabitants of this oblate spheroid on which we move, breathe and suffer for lack of beer. There seems to be a feeling in many quarters that if we could get speech with the Martians, let us say, we might learn from them something to our advantage. There is a disposition to concede the superiority of the fellows Out There...just as some Americans capitulate without a struggle to poets from England, rugs from Constantinople, song and sausage from Germany, religious enthusiasts from Hindustan and cheese from Switzerland, although they have not tested the goods offered and really lack the discrimination to determine their quality. Almost the only foreign importations that were ever sneezed at in this country were Swedish matches and Spanish influenza.

15 But are the Martians...if Martians there be...any more capable than the persons dwelling between the Woolworth Building and the Golden Horn, between Shwe Dagon and the First Church, Scientist, in Boston, Mass.? Perhaps the Martians yearn toward earth, romantically, poetically, the Romeos swearing by its light to the Juliets; the idealists and philosophers fabling that already there exists upon it an ALMOST PERFECT STATE—and now and then a wan prophet lifting his heart to its gleams, as a cup to be filled from Heaven with fresh waters of hope and courage. For this earth, it is also a star.

16 We know they are wrong about us, the lovers in the far stars, the philosophers, poets, the prophets…or are they wrong?

17 They are both right and wrong, as we are probably both right and wrong about them. If we tumbled into Mars or Arcturus of Sirius this evening we should find the people there discussing the shimmy, the jazz, the inconstancy of cooks and the iniquity of retail butchers, no doubt…and they would be equally disappointed by the way we flitter, frivol, flutter and flivver.

18 And yet, that other thing would be there too…that thing that made them look at our star as a symbol of grace and beauty.

19 Men could not think of THE ALMOST PERFECT STATE if they did not have it in them ultimately to create THE ALMOST PERFECT STATE.

20 We used sometimes to walk over the Brooklyn Bridge, that song in stone and steel of an engineer who was also a great artist, at dusk, when the tides of shadow flood in from the lower bay to break in a surf of glory and mystery and illusion against the tall towers of Manhattan. Seen from the middle arch of the bridge at twilight, New York with its girdle of shifting waters and its drift of purple cloud and its quick pulsations of unstable light is a miracle of splendor and beauty that lights up the heart like the laughter of a god.

21 But, descend. Go down into the city. Mingle with the details. The dirty old shed from which the "L" trains and trolleys put out with their jammed and mangled thousands for flattest Flatbush and the unknown bourne of ulterior Brooklyn is still the same dirty old shed; on a hot, damp night the pasty streets stink like a paper-hanger's overalls; you are trodden and over-ridden by greasy little profiteers and their hopping victims; you are encompassed round about by the ugly and the sordid, and the objectionable is exuded upon you from a myriad candid pores; your elation and your illusion vanish like ingenuous snowflakes that have kissed a hot dog

sandwich on its fiery brow, and you say: "Beauty? Aw, h—l! What's the use?"

22 And yet you have seen beauty. And beauty that was created by these people and people like these…You have seen the tall towers of Manhattan, wonderful under the stars. How did it come about that such growths came from such soil—that a breed lawless and sordid and prosaic has written such a mighty hieroglyphic against the sky? This glamor out of a pigsty…how come? How is it that this hideous, half-brute city is also beautiful and a fit habitation for demi-gods? How come?

23 It comes about because the wise and subtle deities permit nothing worthy to be lost. It was with no thought of beauty that the builders labored; no conscious thought; they were masters or slaves in the bitter wars of commerce, and they never saw as a whole what they were making; no one of them did. But each one had had his dream. And the baffled dreams and the broken visions and the ruined hopes and the secret desires of each one labored with him as he labored; the things that were lost and beaten and trampled down went into the stone and steel and gave it soul; the aspiration denied and the hope abandoned and the vision defeated were the things that lived, and not the apparent purpose for which each one of all the millions sweat and toiled or cheated; the hidden things, the silent things, the winged things, so weak they are easily killed, the unacknowledged things, the rejected beauty, the strangled appreciation, the inchoate art, the submerged spirit—these groped and found each other and gathered themselves together and worked themselves into the tiles and mortar of the edifice and made a town that is a worthy fellow of the sunrise and the sea winds.

24 Humanity triumphs over its details.

25 The individual aspiration is always defeated of its perfect fruition and expression, but it is never lost; it passes into the conglomerate being of the race.

26 The way to encourage yourself about the human race is to look at it first from a distance; look at the lights on the high spots. Coming closer, you will be profoundly discouraged at the number of low spots, not to say two-spots. Coming still closer, you will become discouraged once more by the reflection that the same stuff that is in the high spots is also in the two-spots.

» (1921)

On Going a Journey

William Hazlitt

1   One of the pleasantest things in the world is going a journey; but I like to do it myself. I can enjoy society in a room; but out of doors, nature is company for me. I am then never less alone than when alone.

"The fields his study, nature was his book."

2   I cannot see the wit of walking and talking at the same time. When I am in the country, I wish to vegetate like the country. I am not for criticizing hedge-rows and black cattle. I go out of town in order to forget the town and all that is in it. There are those who for this purpose go to watering-places and carry the metropolis with them. I like more elbow-room and fewer incumbrances. I like solitude, when I give myself up to it, for the sake of solitude; nor do I ask for

"a friend in my retreat
Whom I may whisper, solitude is sweet."

3   The soul of a journey is liberty, perfect liberty, to think, feel, do just as one pleases. We go a journey chiefly to be free of all impediments and of all inconveniences; to leave ourselves behind, much more to get rid of others. It is because I want a little breathing-space to muse on indifferent matters, where Contemplation

"May plume her feathers and let grow her wings,
That in the various bustle of resort
Were all too ruffled, and sometimes impair'd,"

4   that I absent myself from the town for awhile, without feeling at a loss the moment I am left by myself. Instead of a friend in a post-chaise or in a Tilbury, to exchange good things with and vary the same stale topics over again, for once let me have a truce with impertinence. Give me the clear blue sky over my head, and the green turf beneath my feet, a winding road before me, and a three hours' march to dinner -- and then to thinking! It is hard if I

cannot start some game on these lone heaths. I laugh, I run, I leap, I sing for joy. From the point of yonder rolling cloud, I plunge into my past being and revel there, as the sunburnt Indian plunges headlong into the wave that wafts him to his native shore. Then long-forgotten things like "sunken wrack and sumless treasuries," burst upon my eager sight, and I begin to feel, think, and be myself again. Instead of an awkward silence, broken by attempts at wit or dull common-places, mine is that undisturbed silence of the heart which alone is perfect eloquence.

5 No one likes puns, alliterations, antitheses, argument, and analysis better than I do; but I sometimes had rather be without them. "Leave, oh, leave me to my repose!" I have just now other business in hand which would seem idle to you, but is with me "very stuff of the conscience." Is not this wild rose sweet without a comment? Does not this daisy leap to my heart set in its coat of emerald? Yet if I were to explain to you the circumstance that has so endeared it to me, you would only smile. Had I not better then keep it to myself, and let it serve me to brood over, from hear to yonder craggy point, and from thence onward to the far-distant horizon? I should be but bad company all that way, and therefore prefer being alone. I have heard it said that you may, when the moody fit comes on, walk or ride on by yourself and indulge your reveries. But this looks like a breach of manners, a neglect of others, and you are thinking all the time that you ought to rejoin your party. "Out upon such half-faced fellowship," say I. I like to be either entirely to myself, or entirely at the disposal of others; to talk or be silent, to walk or sit still, to be sociable or solitary.

6 I was pleased with an observation of Mr Cobbett's that "he thought it a bad French custom to drink our wine with our meals, and that an Englishman ought to do only one thing at a time." So I cannot talk and think, or indulge in melancholy musing and lively conversation by fits and starts. "Let me have a companion of my way," says Sterne, "were it but to remark how the shadows lengthen as the

sun declines." It is beautifully said; but in my opinion, this continual comparing of notes interferes with the involuntary impression of things upon the mind and hurts the sentiment. If you only hint what you feel in a kind of dumb show, it is insipid; if you have to explain it, it is making a toil of a pleasure. You cannot read the book of nature without being perpetually put to the trouble of translating it for the benefit of others.

7   I am for the synthetical method on a journey, in preference to the analytical. I am content to lay in a stock of ideas then, and to examine and anatomize them afterwards. I want to see my vague notions float like the down of the thistle before the breeze, and not to have them entangled in the briars and thorns of controversy. For once, I like to have it all my own way; and this is impossible unless you are alone, or in such company as I do not covet. I have no objection to argue a point with anyone for twenty miles of measured road, but not for pleasure.

8   If you remark the scent of a bean-field crossing the road, perhaps your fellow-traveller has no smell. If you point to a distant object, perhaps he is short-sighted, and has to take out his glass to look at it. There is a feeling in the air, a tone in the colour of a cloud which hits your fancy, but the effect of which you are unable to account for. There is then no sympathy, but an uneasy craving after it, and a dissatisfaction which pursues you on the way, and in the end probably produces ill humour.

9   Now I never quarrel with myself, and take all my own conclusions for granted till I find it necessary to defend them against objections. It is not merely that you may not be of accord on the objects and circumstances that present themselves before you -- these may recall a number of objects and lead to associations too delicate and refined to be possibly communicated to others. Yet these I love to cherish, and sometimes still fondly clutch them, when I can escape from the throng to do so.

10 To give way to our feelings before company, seems extravagance or

affectation; and, on the other hand, to have to unravel this mystery of our being at every turn, and to make others take an equal interest in it (otherwise the end is not answered) is a task to which few are competent. We must "give it an understanding but no tongue." My old friend ... [Coleridge], however, could do both. He could go on in the most delightful explanatory way over hill and dale a summer's day, and convert a landscape into a didactic poem or a Pindaric ode. "He talked far above singing."

11 If I could so clothe my ideas in sounding and flowing words, I might perhaps wish to have some one with me to admire the swelling theme; or I could be more content, were is possible for me still to hear his echoing voice in the woods of All-Foxden. They had "that fine madness in them which our first poets had"; and if they could have been caught by some rare instrument, would have breathed such strains as the following:

"Here be woods as green
As any, air likewise as fresh and sweet
As then smooth Zephyrus plays on the fleet
Face of the curled streams, with flow'rs as many
As the young spring gives, and as choice as any;
Here be all new delights, cool streams and wells,
Arbours o'ergrown with woodbine, caves and dells;
Choose where thou wilt; whilst I sit by and sing.
Or gather rushes, to make many a ring
For thy long fingers; tell thee tales of love;
How the pale Phoebe, hunting in a grove,
First saw the boy Endymion, from whose eyes
She took eternal fire that never dies;
How she convey'd him softly in a sleep,
His temples bound with poppy, to the steep
Head of old Latmos, where she stoops each night,
Gilding the mountain with her brother's light,

Too kiss her sweetest."

Fletcher's Faithful Shepherdess.

12 Had I words and images at command like these, I would attempt to wake the thoughts that lie slumbering on golden ridges in the evening clouds; but at the sight of nature my fancy, poor as it is, droops and closes up its leaves, like flowers at sunset. I can make nothing out on the spot:--I must have time to collect myself.

13 In general, a good thing spoils out-of-door prospects; it should be reserved for table-talk. ... [Lamb] is for this reason, I take it, the worst company in the world out of doors; because he is the best within. I grant, there is one subject on which it is pleasant to talk on a journey; and that is, what one shall have for supper when we get to our inn at night. The open air improves this sort of conversation or friendly altercation by setting a keener edge on appetite. Every mile of the road heightens the flavour of the viands we expect at the end of it. How fine is it to enter some old town, walled and turreted, just at approach of nightfall, or to come to some straggling village, with the lights streaming through the surrounding gloom; and then after inquiring for the best entertainment that the place affords, to "take one's ease at one's inn!" These eventful moments in our lives' history are too precious, too full of solid, heart-felt happiness to be frittered and dribbled away in imperfect sympathy. I would have them all to myself, and drain them to the last drop; they will do to talk of or to write about afterwards. What a delicate speculation it is, after drinking whole goblets of tea,

"The cups that cheer, but not inebriate,"

14 And letting the fumes ascend into the brain, to sit considering what we shall have for supper -- eggs and a rasher, a rabbit smothered in onions, or an excellent veal-cutlet! Sancho in such a situation once fixed upon cow-heel; and his choice, though he could not help it, is not to be disparaged. Then, in the intervals of pictured scenery and Shandean contemplation, to catch the preparation and the stir in the kitchen [getting ready for the gentleman in the parlour]3

Procul, O procul este profani! These hours are sacred to silence and to musing, to be treasured up in the memory, and to feed the source of smiling thoughts hereafter. I would not waste them in idle talk; or if I must have the integrity of fancy broken in upon, I would rather it were by a stranger than a friend. A stranger takes his hue and character from the time and place; he is a part of the furniture and costume of an inn. If he is a Quaker, or from the West Riding of Yorkshire, so much the better. I do not even try to sympathize with him, and he breaks no squares. [How I love to see the camps of the gypsies, and to sigh my soul into that sort of life. If I express this feeling to another, he may qualify and spoil it with some objection.]4 I associate nothing with my travelling companion but present objects and passing events. In his ignorance of me and my affairs, I in a manner forget myself. But a friend reminds one of other things, rips up old grievances, and destroys the abstraction of the scene. He comes in ungraciously between us and our imaginary character. Something is dropped in the course of conversation that gives a hint of your profession and pursuits; or from having some one with you that knows the less sublime portions of your history, it seems that other people do. You are no longer a citizen of the world: but your "unhoused free condition is put into circumspection and confine." The incognito of an inn is one of its striking privileges -- "Lord of one's self, uncumber'd with a name." Oh! It is great to shake off the trammels of the world and of public opinion -- to lose our importunate, tormenting, everlasting personal identity in the elements of nature, and become the creature of the moment, clear of all ties -- to hold to the universe only by a dish of sweet-breads, and to owe nothing but the score of the evening -- and no longer seeking for the applause and meeting with contempt, to be known by no other title than the Gentleman in the parlour! One may take one's choice of all characters in this romantic state of uncertainly as to one's real pretensions, and become indefinitely respectable and negatively right-worshipful. We baffle prejudice and disappoint conjecture; and from being so to others, begin to be objects of curiosity and wonder even to ourselves. We are no more those hackneyed common-places that we appear in the world; an inn restores us to the level of nature and quits scores with society! I have certainly spent some enviable hours at inns -- sometimes when I have been left entirely to myself and have tired to solve some metaphysical problem, as once at Witham-common, where I found out the proof that likenesss is not a case of the association of ideas -- at other times, when there have been pictures in the room, as at St Neot's (I think I was), where I first met with Gribelin's engravings of the Cartoons, into which I entered at once, and at a little inn on the borders of Wales, where there happened to be hanging some of Westall's drawings, which I compared triumphantly (for a theory that I had, not for the admired artist) with the figure of a girl who had ferried me over the Severn, standing up in a boat between me and the twilight -- at other times I might mention luxuriating in books, with a peculiar interest in this way, as I remember sitting up half the night to read Paul and Virgiria , which I picked up at an inn at Bridgewater, after being drenched in the rain all day; and at the same place I got through two volumes of Madam D'Arblay's Camilla . It was on the 10th of April, 1798, that I sat down to a volume of the New Eloise, at the inn at Llangollen, over a bottle of sherry and cold chicken. The letter I chose was that in which St. Preux describes his feelings as he first caught a glimpse from the heights of the Jura of the Pays de Vaud, which I had brought with me as a bon bouche to crown the evening with. It was my birth-day, and I had for the first time comer from a place in the neighbourhood to visit this delightful spot. The road to Llangollen turns off between Chirk and Wrexham; and on passing a certain point you come all at once upon the valley, which opens like an amphitheatre, broad, barren hills rising in majestic state on either side, with "green upland swells that echo to the bleat of flocks" below, and the river Dee babbling over its stony bed in the midst of them. The valley at this time "glittered green with sunny showers," and a budding ash-tree dipped its tender branches in the chiding stream. How proud, how glad I was to walk along the high road that overlooks the delicious prospect, repeating the lines which I have just quoted from Mr Coleridge's poems! But besides the prospect which opened beneath my feet, another also opened to my inward sight, a heavenly vision, on which were written, in letters large as Hope could make them, these four words, Liberty, Genius, Love, Virtue; which have since faded in the light of common day or mock my idle gaze.

"The Beautiful is vanished, and returns not."

15 Still I would return some time or other to this enchanted spot; but I would return to it alone. What other self could I find to share that influx of thoughts of regret and delight, the fragments of which I could hardly conjure up myself, so much have they been broken and defaced! I could stand on some tall rock and over look the precipice of years that separates me from what I then was. I was at that time going shortly to visit the poet whom I have above named. Where is he now? Not only I myself have changed; the world, which was then new to me, has become old and incorrigible. Yet will I turn to thee in thought, O sylvan Dee, in joy, in youth and gladness as though then wert; and thou shalt always be to me the river of Paradise, where I will drink the waters of life freely!

16 There is hardly anything that shows the short-sightedness or capriciousness of the imagination more than travelling does. With change of place we change our ideas; nay . our opinions and feelings. We can by an effort indeed transport ourselves to old and long-forgotten scenes, and then the picture of the mind revives again; but we forget those that we have just left. It seems that we can think but of one place at a time. The canvas of the fancy is but of a certain extent, and if we paint one set of objects upon it, they immediately efface every other. We cannot enlarge our conceptions, we can only shift our point of view. The landscape bares its bosom to the enraptured eye, we take our fill of it and seem as if we could form no other image of beauty or grandeur. We pass on and think no more

of it; the horizon that shuts if from our sight, also blots it from our memory like a dream. In travelling through a wild, barren country, I can form no idea of a woody and cultivated one. It appears to me that all the world must be barren, like what I see of it. In the country we forget the town and in the town we despise the country. "Beyond Hyde Park," says Sir Fopling Flutter, "all is a desert." All that part of the map which we do not see before us is a blank. The world in our conceit of it is not much bigger than a nutshell. It is not one prospect expanded into another, country joined to country, kingdom to kingdom, land to seas, making an image voluminous and vast; --the mind can form no larger idea of space than the eye can take in at a single glance. The rest is a name written in a map, a calculation of arithmetic. For instance, what is the true signification of that immense mass of territory and population, known by the name of China to us? An inch of pasteboard on a wooden globe, of no more account than a China orange! Things near us are seen at the size of life; things at a distance are diminished to the size of the understanding. We measure the universe by ourselves, and even comprehend the texture of our own being only peace-meal. In this way, however, we remember an infinity of things and places. The mind is like a mechanical instrument that plays a great variety of tunes, but it must play them in succession. One idea recalls another, but it at the same times excludes all others. In trying to renew old recollections, we cannot as it were unfold the whole web of our existence; we must pick out the single threads. So in coming to a place where we have formerly lived and with which we have intimate associations, every one must have found that the feeling grows more vivid the nearer we approach the spot, from the mere anticipation of the actual impression; we remember circumstances, feelings, persons, faces, names that we had not thought of for years; but for the time all the rest of the world is forgotten! -- To return to the question I have quitted above:

17 I have no objection to go to see ruins, aqueducts, pictures, in

company with a friend or a party, bur rather the contrary, for the former reason reversed. They are intelligible matters and will bear talking about. The sentiment here is not tacit, but communicable and overt. Salisbury Plain is barren of criticism, but Stonehenge will bear a discussion antiquarian, picturesque, and philosophical. In setting out on a party of pleasure, the first consideration is always where we shall go to, in taking a solitary ramble, the question is what we shall meet with by the way. "The mind is its own place"; nor are we anxious to arrive at the end of our journey. I can myself do the honours indifferently well to works or art and curiosity. I once took a party to Oxford with no mean Å©clat -- showed them the seat of the Muses at a distance

"With glistering spires and pinnacles adorn'd----"

18 descanted on the learned air that breathes from the grassy quadrangles and stone walls of halls and colleges -- was at home in the Bodleian; and at Blenheim quite superseded the powered Cicerone that attended us, and that pointed in vain with his wand to commonplace beauties in matchless pictures. -- As another exception to the above reasoning, I should not feel confident in venturing on a journey in a foreign country without a companion. I should want at intervals to hear the sound of my own language. There is an involuntary antipathy in the mind of an Englishmen to foreign manners and notions that requires the assistance of social sympathy to carry it off. As the distance from home increases, this relief, which was at first a luxury, becomes a passion and an appetite. A person would almost feel stifled to find himself in the deserts of Arabia without friends and countrymen; there must be allowed to be something in the view of Athens or old Rome that claims the utterance of speech; and I own that the Pyramids are too mighty for any single contemplation. In such situations, so opposite to all one's ordinary train of ideas, one seems a species by one's self, a limb torn off from society, unless one can meet with instant fellowship and support. -- Yet I did not feel this want or craving very pressing

once, when I first set foot on the laughing shores of France. Calais was peopled with novelty and delight. The confused, busy murmur of the place was like oil and wine poured into my ears; nor did the mariner's hymn, which was sung from the top of an old crazy vessel in the harbour, as the sun went down, send a alien sound into my soul. I only breathed the air of general humanity. I walked over "the vine-covered hills and gay regions of France," erect and satisfied; for the image of man was not cast down and chained to the foot of arbitrary thrones; I was at no loss for language, for that of all the great schools of painting was open to me. The whole is vanished like a shade. Pictures, heroes, glory, freedom, all are fled; nothing remains but the Bourbons and the French People! -- There is undoubtedly a sensation in travelling into foreign parts that is to be had nowhere else; but it is more pleasing at the time than lasting. It is too remote from our habitual associations to be a common topic of discourse or reference, and, like a dream of another state of existence, does not piece into our daily modes of life. It is an animated but a momentary hallucination. It demands an effort to exchange our actual for our ideal identity; and to feel the pulse of our old transports revive very keenly, we must "jump" all our present comforts and connexions. Our romantic and itinerant character is not to be domesticated. Dr. Johnson remarked how little foreign travel added to the facilities of conversation in those who had been abroad. In fact, the time we have spent there is both delightful and in one sense, instructive; but it appears to be cut out of our substantial, downright existence, and never to join kindly on to it. We are not the same, but another, and perhaps more enviable individual, all the time we are out of our own country. We are lost to ourselves, as well as our friends. So the poet somewhat quaintly sings,

"Out of my country and myself I go."

19 Those who wish to forget painful thoughts, do well to absent themselves of a while from the ties and objects that recall them; but we

can be said only to fulfil our destiny in the place that gave us birth. I should on this account like well enough to spend the whole of my life in travelling abroad, if I could anywhere borrow another life to spend afterwards at home!

»   (1822)

Getting Up On Cold Mornings

by Leigh Hunt

1   An Italian author–Giulio Cordara, a Jesuit–has written a poem upon insects, which he begins by insisting, that those troublesome and abominable little animals were created for our annoyance, and that they were certainly not inhabitants of Paradise. We of the north may dispute this piece of theology; but on the other hand, it is clear as the snow on the house-tops, that Adam was not under the necessity of shaving; and that when Eve walked out of her delicious bower, she did not step upon ice three inches thick.

2   Some people say it is a very easy thing to get up of a cold morning. You have only, they tell you, to take the resolution; and the thing is done. This may be very true; just as a boy at school has only to take a flogging, and the thing is over. But we have not at all made up our minds upon it; and we find it a very pleasant exercise to discuss the matter, candidly, before we get up. This at least is not idling, though it may be lying. It affords an excellent answer to those, who ask how lying in bed can be indulged in by a reasoning being,–a rational creature. How? Why with the argument calmly at work in one's head, and the clothes over one's shoulder. Oh–it is a fine way of spending a sensible, impartial half-hour.

3   If these people would be more charitable, they would get on with their argument better. But they are apt to reason so ill, and to assert so dogmatically, that one could wish to have them stand round one's bed of a bitter morning, and lie before their faces. They ought to hear both sides of the bed, the inside and out. If they cannot entertain themselves with their own thoughts for half an hour or so, it is not the fault of those who can. If their will is never pulled aside by the enticing arms of imagination, so much the luckier for the stage-coachman.

4   Candid inquiries into one's decumbency, besides the greater or

less privileges to be allowed a man in proportion to his ability of keeping early hours, the work given his faculties, etc., will at least concede their due merits to such representations as the following. In the first place, says the injured but calm appealer, I have been warm all night, and find my system in a state perfectly suitable to a warm-blooded animal. To get out of this state into the cold, besides the inharmonious and uncritical abruptness of the transition, is so unnatural to such a creature, that the poets, refining upon the tortures of the damned, make one of their greatest agonies consist in being suddenly transported from heat to cold,–from fire to ice. They are "haled" out of their "beds," says Milton, by "harpy-footed furies,"–fellows who come to call them. On my first movement towards the anticipation of getting up, I find that such parts of the sheets and bolster, as are exposed to the air of the room, are stone-cold. On opening my eyes, the first thing that meets them is my own breath rolling forth, as if in the open air, like smoke out of a cottage chimney. Think of this symptom. Then I turn my eyes sideways and see the window all frozen over. Think of that. Then the servant comes in. "It is very cold this morning, is it not?"–"Very cold, Sir."–"Very cold indeed, isn't it?"–"Very cold indeed, Sir."–"More than usually so, isn't it, even for this weather?" (Here the servant's wit and good-nature are put to a considerable test, and the inquirer lies on thorns for the answer.) "Why, Sir … I think it is." (Good creature! There is not a better, or more truth-telling servant going.) "I must rise, however–get me some warm water."–Here comes a fine interval between the departure of the servant and the arrival of the hot water; during which, of course, it is of "no use" to get up. The hot water comes. "Is it quite hot?"–"Yes, Sir."–"Perhaps too hot for shaving: I must wait a little?"–"No, Sir; it will just do." (There is an over-nice propriety sometimes, an officious zeal of virtue, a little troublesome.) "Oh–the shirt–you must air my clean shirt;–linen gets very damp this weather."–"Yes, Sir." Here another delicious five minutes. A knock at the door. "Oh, the shirt–very well. My stock-ings–I think the stockings had better be aired too."–"Very well,

Sir."–Here another interval. At length everything is ready, except myself. I now, continues our incumbent (a happy word, by the bye, for a country vicar)–I now cannot help thinking a good deal–who can?–upon the unnecessary and villainous custom of shaving: it is a thing so unmanly (here I nestle closer)–so effeminate (here I recoil from an unlucky step into the colder part of the bed.)–No wonder that the Queen of France took part with the rebels against the degenerate King, her husband, who first affronted her smooth visage with a face like her own. The Emperor Julian never showed the luxuriancy of his genius to better advantage than in reviving the flowing beard. Look at Cardinal Bembo's picture–at Michael Angelo's–at Titian's–at Shakespeare's–at Fletcher's–at Spenser's–at Chaucer's–at Alfred's–at Plato's–I could name a great man for every tick of my watch.–Look at the Turks, a grave and otiose people.–Think of Haroun Al Raschid and Bed-ridden Hassan.–Think of Wortley Montagu, the worthy son of his mother, a man above the prejudice of his time.–Look at the Persian gentlemen, whom one is ashamed of meeting about the suburbs, their dress and appearance are so much finer than our own.–Lastly, think of the razor itself–how totally opposed to every sensation of bed–how cold, how edgy, how hard! how utterly different from anything like the warm and circling amplitude, which

> Sweetly recommends itself
> Unto our gentle senses.

5 Add to this, benumbed fingers, which may help you to cut yourself, a quivering body, a frozen towel, and a ewer full of ice; and he that says there is nothing to oppose in all this, only shows, at any rate, that he has no merit in opposing it.

6 Thomson the poet, who exclaims in his Seasons–Falsely luxurious! Will not man awake? used to lie in bed till noon, because he said he had no motive in getting up. He could imagine the good of rising; but then he could also imagine the good of lying still; and his exclamation, it must be allowed, was made upon summer-time, not winter.

We must proportion the argument to the individual character. A money-getter may be drawn out of his bed by three and four pence; but this will not suffice for a student. A proud man may say, "What shall I think of myself, if I don't get up?" but the more humble one will be content to waive this prodigious notion of himself, out of respect to his kindly bed. The mechanical man shall get up without any ado at all; and so shall the barometer. An ingenious lier in bed will find hard matter of discussion even on the score of health and longevity. He will ask us for our proofs and precedents of the ill effects of lying later in cold weather; and sophisticate much on the advantages of an even temperature of body; of the natural propensity (pretty universal) to have one's way; and of the animals that roll themselves up, and sleep all the winter. As to longevity, he will ask whether the longest life is of necessity the best; and whether Holborn is the handsomest street in London.

7   We only know of one confounding, not to say confounded argument, fit to overturn the huge luxury, the "enormous bliss"–of the vice in question. A lier in bed may be allowed to profess a disinterested indifference for his health or longevity; but while he is showing the reasonableness of consulting his own or one person's comfort, he must admit the proportionate claim of more than one; and the best way to deal with him is this, especially for a lady; for we earnestly recommend the use of that sex on such occasions, if not somewhat over-persuasive; since extremes have an awkward knack of meeting. First then, admit all the ingeniousness of what he says, telling him that the bar has been deprived of an excellent lawyer. Then look at him in the most good-natured manner in the world, with a mixture of assent and appeal in your countenance, and tell him that you are waiting breakfast for him; that you never like to breakfast without him; that you really want it too; that the servants want theirs; that you shall not know how to get the house into order, unless he rises; and that you are sure he would do things twenty times worse, even than getting out of his warm bed, to put

them all into good humour and a state of comfort. Then, after having said this, throw in the comparatively indifferent matter, to him, about his health; but tell him that it is no indifferent matter to you; that the sight of his illness makes more people suffer than one; but that if, nevertheless, he really does feel so very sleepy and so very much refreshed by— Yet stay; we hardly know whether the frailty of a— Yes, yes; say that too, especially if you say it with sincerity; for if the weakness of human nature on the one hand and the vis inertiae on the other, should lead him to take advantage of it once or twice, good-humour and sincerity form an irresistible junction at last; and are still better and warmer things than pillows and blankets.

8 Other little helps of appeal may be thrown in, as occasion requires. You may tell a lover, for instance, that lying in bed makes people corpulent; a father, that you wish him to complete the fine manly example he sets his children; a lady, that she will injure her bloom or her shape, which M. or W. admires so much; and a student or artist, that he is always so glad to have done a good day's work, in his best manner.

9 Reader. And pray, Mr. Indicator, how do you behave yourself in this respect?

10 Indic. Oh, Madam, perfectly, of course; like all advisers.

11 Reader. Nay, I allow that your mode of argument does not look quite so suspicious as the old way of sermonising and severity, but I have my doubts, especially from that laugh of yours. If I should look in to-morrow morning–

12 Indic. Ah, Madam, the look in of a face like yours does anything with me. It shall fetch me up at nine, if you please–six, I meant to say.

» (1820)

Bachelors

Washington Irving

The Bachelor most joyfully
In pleasant plight doth pass his dales,
Good fellowship and companie
He doth maintain and keep alwaies.

—EVEN'S Old Ballads.

1   There is no character in the comedy of human life that is more difficult to play well, than that of an old Bachelor. When a single gentleman, therefore, arrives at that critical period when he begins to consider it an impertinent question to be asked his age, I would advise him, to look well to his ways. This period, it is true, is much later with some men than with others; I have witnessed more than once the meeting of two wrinkled old lads of this kind, who had not seen each other for several years, and have been amused by the amicable exchange of compliments on each other's appearance, that takes place on such occasions. There is always one invariable observation: "Why, bless my soul! you look younger than when I last saw you!" Whenever a man's friends begin to compliment him about looking young, he may be sure that they think he is growing old.

2   I am led to make these remarks by the conduct of Master Simon and the general, who have become great cronies. As the former is the younger by many years, he is regarded as quite a youthful blade by the general, who moreover looks upon him as a man of great wit and prodigious acquirements. I have already hinted that Master Simon is a family beau, and considered rather a young fellow by all the elderly ladies of the connexion; for an old bachelor, in an old family connexion, is something like an actor in a regular dramatic corps, who seems to "flourish in immortal youth," and will continue to play the Romeos and Rangers for half a century together.

3   Master Simon, too, is a little of the chameleon, and takes a different hue with every different companion: he is very attentive and officious, and somewhat sentimental, with Lady Lillycraft; copies out little namby-pamby ditties and love-songs for her, and draws quivers, and doves, and darts, and Cupids, to be worked on the corners of her pocket-handkerchiefs. He indulges, however, in very considerable latitude with the other married ladies of the family; and has many sly pleasantries to whisper to them, that provoke an equivocal laugh and a tap of the fan. But when he gets among young company, such as Frank Bracebridge, the Oxonian, and the general, he is apt to put on the mad wag, and to talk in a very bachelor-like strain about the sex.

4   In this he has been encouraged by the example of the general, whom he looks up to as a man who has seen the world. The general, in fact, tells shocking stories after dinner, when the ladies have retired, which he gives as some of the choice things that are served up at the Mulligatawney club; a knot of boon companions in London. He also repeats the fat jokes of old Major Pendergast, the wit of the club, and which, though the general can hardly repeat them for laughing, always make Mr. Bracebridge look grave, he having a great antipathy to an indecent jest. In a word, the general is a complete instance of the declension in gay life, by which a young man of pleasure is apt to cool down into an obscene old gentleman.

5   I saw him and Master Simon, an evening or two since, conversing with a buxom milkmaid in a meadow; and from their elbowing each other now and then, and the general's shaking his shoulders, blowing up his cheeks, and breaking out into a short fit of irrepressible laughter, I had no doubt they were playing the mischief with the girl.

6   As I looked at them through a hedge, I could not but think they would have made a tolerable group for a modern picture of Susannah and the two elders. It is true, the girl seemed in nowise alarmed at the force of the enemy; and I question, had either of them been

alone, whether she would not have been more than they would have ventured to encounter. Such veteran roysters are daring wags when together, and will put any female to the blush with their jokes; but they are as quiet as lambs when they fall singly into the clutches of a fine woman.

7   In spite of the general's years, he evidently is a little vain of his person, and ambitious of conquests. I have observed him on Sunday in church, eyeing the country girls most suspiciously; and have seen him leer upon them with a downright amorous look, even when he has been gallanting Lady Lillycraft, with great cere-mony, through the church-yard. The general, in fact, is a veteran in the service of Cupid, rather than of Mars, having signalized himself in all the garrison towns and country quarters, and seen service in every ball-room of England. Not a celebrated beauty but he has laid siege to; and if his word may be taken in a matter wherein no man is apt to be over-veracious, it is incredible the success he has had with the fair. At present he is like a worn-out warrior, retired from service; but who still cocks his beaver with a military air, and talks stoutly of fighting whenever he comes within the smell of gunpowder.

8   I have heard him speak his mind very freely over his bottle, about the folly of the captain in taking a wife; as he thinks a young soldier should care for nothing but his "bottle and kind landlady." But, in fact, he says the service on the continent has had a sad effect upon the young men; they have been ruined by light wines and French quadrilles. "They've nothing," he says, "of the spirit of the old service. There are none of your six-bottle men left, that were the souls of a mess dinner, and used to play the very deuce among the women."

9   As to a bachelor, the general affirms that he is a free and easy man, with no baggage to take care of but his portmanteau; but a married man, with his wife hanging on his arm, always puts him in mind of a chamber candlestick, with its extinguisher hitched to it. I should

hot mind all this, if it were merely confined to the general; but I fear he will be the ruin of my friend, Master Simon, who already begins to echo his heresies, and to talk in the style of a gentleman that has seen life, and lived upon the town. Indeed, the general seems to have taken Master Simon in hand, and talks of showing him the lions when he comes to town, and of introducing him to a knot of choice spirits at the Mulligatawney club; which, I understand, is composed of old nabobs, officers in the Company's employ, and other "men of Ind," that have seen service in the East, and returned home burnt out with curry, and touched with the liver complaint. They have their regular club, where they eat Mulligatawney soup, smoke the hookah, talk about Tippoo Saib, Seringapatam, and tiger-hunting; and are tediously agreeable in each other's company.

»   (1822)

Dream-Children, A Revery

By Charles Lamb

1   Children love to listen to stories about their elders, when they were children; to stretch their imagination to the conception of a traditionary great-uncle or grandame, whom they never saw. It was in this spirit that my little ones crept about me the other evening to hear about their great-grandmother Field, who lived in a great house in Norfolk (a hundred times bigger than that in which they and papa lived) which had been the scene—so at least it was generally believed in that part of the country—of the tragic incidents which they had lately become familiar with from the ballad of the Children in the Wood.

2   Certain it is that the whole story of the children and their cruel uncle was to be seen fairly carved out in wood upon the chimney-piece of the great hall, the whole story down to the Robin Redbreasts, till a foolish rich person pulled it down to set up a marble one of modern invention in its stead, with no story upon it.

3   Here Alice put out one of her dear mother's looks, too tender to be called upbraiding. Then I went on to say, how religious and how good their great-grandmother Field was, how beloved and respected by everybody, though she was not indeed the mistress of this great house, but had only the charge of it (and yet in some respects she might be said to be the mistress of it too) committed to her by the owner, who preferred living in a newer and more fashionable mansion which he had purchased somewhere in the adjoining county; but still she lived in it in a manner as if it had been her own, and kept up the dignity of the great house in a sort while she lived, which afterward came to decay, and was nearly pulled down, and all its old ornaments stripped and carried away to the owner's other house, where they were set up, and looked as awkward as if some one were to carry away the old tombs they had

seen lately at the Abbey, and stick them up in Lady C.'s tawdry gilt drawing-room.

4   Here John smiled, as much as to say, "that would be foolish indeed." And then I told how, when she came to die, her funeral was attended by a concourse of all the poor, and some of the gentry too, of the neighborhood for many miles round, to show their respect for her memory, because she had been such a good and religious woman; so good indeed that she knew all the Psaltery by heart, aye, and a great part of the Testament besides.

5   Here little Alice spread her hands. Then I told what a tall, upright, graceful person their great-grandmother Field once was; and how in her youth she was esteemed the best dancer—here Alice's little right foot played an involuntary movement, till upon my looking grave, it desisted—the best dancer, I was saying, in the county, till a cruel disease, called a cancer, came, and bowed her down with pain; but it could never bend her good spirits, or make them stoop, but they were still upright, because she was so good and religious.

6   Then I told how she was used to sleep by herself in a lone chamber of the great lone house; and how she believed that an apparition of two infants was to be seen at midnight gliding up and down the great staircase near where she slept, but she said "those innocents would do her no harm"; and how frightened I used to be, though in those days I had my maid to sleep with me, because I was never half so good or religious as she—and yet I never saw the infants.

7   Here John expanded all his eyebrows and tried to look courageous. Then I told how good she was to all her grand-children, having us to the great house in the holidays, where I in particular used to spend many hours by myself, in gazing upon the old busts of the Twelve Cæsars, that had been Emperors of Rome, till the old marble heads would seem to live again, or I to be turned into marble with them; how I never could be tired with roaming about that huge mansion, with its vast empty rooms, with their worn-out hangings, fluttering tapestry, and carved oaken panels, with the gild-

ing almost rubbed out—sometimes in the spacious old-fashioned gardens, which I had almost to myself, unless when now and then a solitary gardening man would cross me—and how the nectarines and peaches hung upon the walls, without my ever offering to pluck them, because they were forbidden fruit, unless now and then,—and because I had more pleasure in strolling about among the old melancholy-looking yew trees, or the firs, and picking up the red berries, and the fir apples, which were good for nothing but to look at—or in lying about upon the fresh grass, with all the fine garden smells around me—or basking in the orangery, till I could almost fancy myself ripening, too, along with the oranges and the limes in that grateful warmth—or in watching the dace that darted to and fro in the fish pond, at the bottom of the garden, with here and there a great sulky pike hanging midway down the water in silent state, as if it mocked at their impertinent friskings,—I had more pleasure in these busy-idle diversions than in all the sweet flavors of peaches, nectarines, oranges, and such like common baits of children.

8   Here John slyly deposited back upon the plate a bunch of grapes, which, not unobserved by Alice, he had mediated dividing with her, and both seemed willing to relinquish them for the present as irrelevant. Then, in somewhat a more heightened tone, I told how, though their great-grandmother Field loved all her grand-children, yet in an especial manner she might be said to love their uncle, John L——, because he was so handsome and spirited a youth, and a king to the rest of us; and, instead of moping about in solitary corners, like some of us, he would mount the most mettlesome horse he could get, when but an imp no bigger than themselves, and make it carry him half over the county in a morning, and join the hunters when there were any out—and yet he loved the old great house and gardens too, but had too much spirit to be always pent up within their boundaries —and how their uncle grew up to man's estate as brave as he was handsome, to the admiration of everybody, but of

their great-grandmother Field most especially; and how he used to carry me upon his back when I was a lame-footed boy—for he was a good bit older than me—many a mile when I could not walk for pain;—and how in after life he became lame-footed too, and I did not always (I fear) make allowances enough for him when he was impatient, and in pain, nor remember sufficiently how considerate he had been to me when I was lame-footed; and how when he died, though he had not been dead an hour, it seemed as if he had died a great while ago, such a distance there is betwixt life and death; and how I bore his death as I thought pretty well at first, but afterward it haunted and haunted me; and though I did not cry or take it to heart as some do, and as I think he would have done if I had died, yet I missed him all day long, and knew not till then how much I had loved him. I missed his kindness, and I missed his crossness, and wished him to be alive again, to be quarreling with him (for we quarreled sometimes), rather than not have him again, and was as uneasy without him, as he their poor uncle must have been when the doctor took off his limb.

9 Here the children fell a crying, and asked if their little mourning which they had on was not for uncle John, and they looked up and prayed me not to go on about their uncle, but to tell them some stories about their pretty, dead mother. Then I told them how for seven long years, in hope sometimes, sometimes in despair, yet persisting ever, I courted the fair Alice W———n; and, as much as children could understand, I explained to them what coyness, and difficulty, and denial meant in maidens—when suddenly, turning to Alice, the soul of the first Alice looked out at her eyes with such a reality of re-presentment, that I became in doubt which of them stood there before me, or whose that bright hair was; and while I stood gazing, both the children gradually grew fainter to my view, receding, and still receding till nothing at last but two mournful features were seen in the uttermost distance, which, without speech, strangely impressed upon me the effects of speech: "We are

not of Alice, nor of thee, nor are we children at all. The children of Alice call Bartrum father. We are nothing; less than nothing, and dreams. We are only what might have been, and must wait upon the tedious shores of Lethe millions of ages before we have existence, and a name"—and immediately awaking, I found myself quietly seated in my bachelor armchair, where I had fallen asleep, with the faithful Bridget unchanged by my side—but John L. (or James Elia) was gone forever.

»   (1822)

The Praise of Chimney-Sweepers

Charles Lamb

1   I like to meet a sweep--understand me--not a grown sweeper--old chimney-sweepers are by no means attractive--but one of those tender novices, blooming through their first nigritude, the maternal washings not quite effaced from the cheek--such as come forth with the dawn, or somewhat earlier, with their little professional notes sounding like the _peep peep_ of a young sparrow; or liker to the matin lark should I pronounce them, in their aerial ascents not seldom anticipating the sun-rise?

2   I have a kindly yearning towards these dim specks--poor blots--innocent blacknesses--I reverence these young Africans of our own growth--these almost clergy imps, who sport their cloth without assumption; and from their little pulpits (the tops of chimneys), in the nipping air of a December morning, preach a lesson of patience to mankind.

3   When a child, what a mysterious pleasure it was to witness their operation! to see a chit no bigger than one's-self enter, one knew not by what process, into what seemed the _fauces Averni_--to pursue him in imagination, as he went sounding on through so many dark stifling caverns, horrid shades!--to shudder with the idea that "now, surely, he must be lost for ever!"--to revive at hearing his feeble shout of discovered day-light--and then (O fulness of delight) running out of doors, to come just in time to see the sable phenomenon emerge in safety, the brandished weapon of his art victorious like some flag waved over a conquered citadel! I seem to remember having been told, that a bad sweep was once left in a stack with his brush, to indicate which way the wind blew. It was an awful spectacle certainly; not much unlike the old stage direction in Macbeth, where the "Apparition of a child crowned with a tree in his hand rises."

4　Reader, if thou meetest one of these small gentry in thy early rambles, it is good to give him a penny. It is better to give him two-pence. If it be starving weather, and to the proper troubles of his hard occupation, a pair of kibed heels (no unusual accompaniment) be superadded, the demand on thy humanity will surely rise to a tester.

5　There is a composition, the ground-work of which I have understood to be the sweet wood 'yclept sassafras. This wood boiled down to a kind of tea, and tempered with an infusion of milk and sugar, hath to some tastes a delicacy beyond the China luxury. I know not how thy palate may relish it; for myself, with every deference to the judicious Mr. Read, who hath time out of mind kept open a shop (the only one he avers in London) for the vending of this "wholesome and pleasant beverage, on the south side of Fleet-street, as thou approachest Bridge-street--_the only Salopian house_,"--I have never yet adventured to dip my own particular lip in a basin of his commended ingredients--a cautious premonition to the olfactories constantly whispering to me, that my stomach must infallibly, with all due courtesy, decline it. Yet I have seen palates, otherwise not uninstructed in dietetical elegances, sup it up with avidity.

6　I know not by what particular conformation of the organ it happens, but I have always found that this composition is surprisingly gratifying to the palate of a young chimney-sweeper--whether the oily particles (sassafras is slightly oleaginous) do attenuate and soften the fuliginous concretions, which are sometimes found (in dissections) to adhere to the roof of the mouth in these unfledged practitioners; or whether Nature, sensible that she had mingled too much of bitter wood in the lot of these raw victims, caused to grow out of the earth her sassafras for a sweet lenitive--but so it is, that no possible taste or odour to the senses of a young chimney-sweeper can convey a delicate excitement comparable to this mixture. Being penniless, they will yet hang their black heads over the ascending steam, to gratify one sense if possible, seemingly no less pleased than those domestic animals--cats--when they purr over a new-found sprig of valerian. There is something more in these sympathies than philosophy can inculcate.

7 Now albeit Mr. Read boasteth, not without reason, that his is the _only Salopian house;_ yet be it known to thee, reader--if thou art one who keepest what are called good hours, thou art haply ignorant of the fact--he hath a race of industrious imitators, who from stalls, and under open sky, dispense the same savoury mess to humbler customers, at that dead time of the dawn, when (as extremes meet) the rake, reeling home from his midnight cups, and the hard-handed artisan leaving his bed to resume the premature labours of the day, jostle, not unfrequently to the manifest discon-certing of the former, for the honours of the pavement. It is the time when, in summer, between the expired and the not yet relu-mined kitchen-fires, the kennels of our fair metropolis give forth their least satisfactory odours. The rake, who wisheth to dissipate his o'er-night vapours in more grateful coffee, curses the ungenial fume, as he passeth; but the artisan stops to taste, and blesses the fragrant breakfast.

8 This is _Saloop_--the precocious herb-woman's darling--the delight of the early gardener, who transports his smoking cabbages by break of day from Hammersmith to Covent-garden's famed piazzas--the delight, and, oh I fear, too often the envy, of the unpennied sweep. Him shouldest thou haply encounter, with his dim visage pendent over the grateful steam, regale him with a sumptuous basin (it will cost thee but three half-pennies) and a slice of delicate bread and butter (an added halfpenny)--so may thy culinary fires, eased of the o'er-charged secretions from thy worse-placed hospitalities, curl up a lighter volume to the welkin--so may the descending soot never taint thy costly well-ingredienced soups--nor the odious cry, quick-reaching from street to street, of the _fired chimney_, invite the rattling engines from ten adjacent parishes, to disturb for a casual

scintillation thy peace and pocket!

9   I am by nature extremely susceptible of street affronts; the jeers and taunts of the populace; the low-bred triumph they display over the casual trip, or splashed stocking, of a gentleman. Yet can I endure the jocularity of a young sweep with something more than forgiveness.--In the last winter but one, pacing along Cheapside with my accustomed precipitation when I walk westward, a treacherous slide brought me upon my back in an instant. I scrambled up with pain and shame enough--yet outwardly trying to face it down, as if nothing had happened--when the roguish grin of one of these young wits encountered me. There he stood, pointing me out with his dusky finger to the mob, and to a poor woman (I suppose his mother) in particular, till the tears for the exquisiteness of the fun (so he thought it) worked themselves out at the corners of his poor red eyes, red from many a previous weeping, and soot-inflamed, yet twinkling through all with such a joy, snatched out of desolation, that Hogarth--but Hogarth has got him already (how could he miss him?) in the March to Finchley, grinning at the pye-man- -there he stood, as he stands in the picture, irremovable, as if the jest was to last for ever--with such a maximum of glee, and minimum of mischief, in his mirth--for the grin of a genuine sweep hath absolutely no malice in it--that I could have been content, if the honour of a gentleman might endure it, to have remained his butt and his mockery till midnight.

10 I am by theory obdurate to the seductiveness of what are called a fine set of teeth. Every pair of rosy lips (the ladies must pardon me) is a casket, presumably holding such jewels; but, methinks, they should take leave to "air" them as frugally as possible. The fine lady, or fine gentleman, who show me their teeth, show me bones. Yet must I confess, that from the mouth of a true sweep a display (even to ostentation) of those white and shining ossifications, strikes me as an agreeable anomaly in manners, and an allowable piece of foppery. It is, as when

11 A sable cloud Turns forth her silver lining on the night.

12 It is like some remnant of gentry not quite extinct; a badge of better days; a hint of nobility:--and, doubtless, under the obscuring darkness and double night of their forlorn disguisement, oftentimes lurketh good blood, and gentle conditions, derived from lost ancestry, and a lapsed pedigree. The premature apprenticements of these tender victims give but too much encouragement, I fear, to clandestine, and almost infantile abductions; the seeds of civility and true courtesy, so often discernible in these young grafts (not otherwise to be accounted for) plainly hint at some forced adoptions; many noble Rachels mourning for their children, even in our days, countenance the fact; the tales of fairy-spiriting may shadow a lamentable verity, and the recovery of the young Montagu be but a solitary instance of, good fortune, out of many irreparable and hopeless _defiliations_.

13 In one of the state-beds at Arundel Castle, a few years since--under a ducal canopy--(that seat of the Howards is an object of curiosity to visitors, chiefly for its beds, in which the late duke was especially a connoisseur)--encircled with curtains of delicatest crimson, with starry coronets inwoven--folded between a pair of sheets whiter and softer than the lap where Venus lulled Ascanius--was discovered by chance, after all methods of search had failed, at noonday, fast asleep, a lost chimney-sweeper. The little creature, having somehow confounded his passage among the intricacies of those lordly chimneys, by some unknown aperture had alighted upon this magnificent chamber; and, tired with his tedious explorations, was unable to resist the delicious invitement to repose, which he there saw exhibited; so, creeping between the sheets very quietly, laid his black head upon the pillow, and slept like a young Howard.

14 Such is the account given to the visitors at the Castle.--But I cannot help seeming to perceive a confirmation of what I have just hinted at in this story. A high instinct was at work in the case, or I am mistaken. Is it probable that a poor child of that description, with whatever weariness he might be visited, would have ventured, under such a penalty, as he would be taught to expect, to uncover the sheets of a Duke's bed, and deliberately to lay himself down between them, when the rug, or the carpet, presented an obvious couch, still far above his pretensions--is this probable, I would ask, if the great power of nature, which I contend for, had not been manifested within him, prompting to the adventure? Doubtless this young nobleman (for such my mind misgives me that he must be) was allured by some memory, not amounting to full consciousness, of his condition in infancy, when he was used to be lapt by his mother, or his nurse, in just such sheets as he there found, into which he was now but creeping back as into his proper _incunabula_, and resting-place.--By no other theory, than by this sentiment of a pre-existent state (as I may call it), can I explain a deed so venturous, and, indeed, upon any other system, so indecorous, in this tender, but unseasonable, sleeper.

15 My pleasant friend JEM WHITE was so impressed with a belief of metamorphoses like this frequently taking place, that in some sort to reverse the wrongs of fortune in these poor changelings, he instituted an annual feast of chimney-sweepers, at which it was his pleasure to officiate as host and waiter. It was a solemn supper held in Smithfield, upon the yearly return of the fair of St. Bartholomew. Cards were issued a week before to the master-sweeps in and about the metropolis, confining the invitation to their younger fry. Now and then an elderly stripling would get in among us, and be good-naturedly winked at; but our main body were infantry. One unfortunate wight, indeed, who, relying upon his dusky suit, had intruded himself into our party, but by tokens was providentially discovered in time to be no chimney-sweeper (all is not soot which looks so), was quoited out of the presence with universal indignation, as not having on the wedding garment; but in general the greatest harmony prevailed. The place chosen was a convenient spot among the pens, at the north side of the fair,

not so far distant as to be impervious to the agreeable hubbub of that vanity; but remote enough not to be obvious to the interruption of every gaping spectator in it. The guests assembled about seven. In those little temporary parlours three tables were spread with napery, not so fine as substantial, and at every board a comely hostess presided with her pan of hissing sausages. The nostrils of the young rogues dilated at the savour. JAMES WHITE, as head waiter, had charge of the first table; and myself, with our trusty companion BIGOD, ordinarily ministered to the other two. There was clambering and jostling, you may be sure, who should get at the first table--for Rochester in his maddest days could not have done the humours of the scene with more spirit than my friend. After some general expression of thanks for the honour the company had done him, his inaugural ceremony was to clasp the greasy waist of old dame Ursula (the fattest of the three), that stood frying and fretting, half-blessing, half-cursing "the gentleman," and imprint upon her chaste lips a tender salute, whereat the universal host would set up a shout that tore the concave, while hundreds of grinning teeth startled the night with their brightness. O it was a pleasure to see the sable younkers lick in the unctuous meat, with _his_ more unctuous sayings--how he would fit the tit bits to the puny mouths, reserving the lengthier links for the seniors-- how he would intercept a morsel even in the jaws of some young desperado, declaring it "must to the pan again to be browned, for it was not fit for a gentleman's eating"--how he would recommend this slice of white bread, or that piece of kissing-crust, to a tender juvenile, advising them all to have a care of cracking their teeth, which were their best patrimony,--how genteelly he would deal about the small ale, as if it were wine, naming the brewer, and protesting, if it were not good, he should lose their custom; with a special recommendation to wipe the lip before drinking. Then we had our toasts--"The King,"--the "Cloth,"--which, whether they understood or not, was equally diverting and flattering;--and for a crowning sentiment, which never failed, "May the Brush supersede the Laurel!" All these, and fifty other fancies, which were rather felt than comprehended by his guests, would he utter, standing upon tables, and prefacing every sentiment with a "Gentlemen, give me leave to propose so and so," which was a prodigious comfort to those young orphans; every now and then stuffing into his mouth (for it did not do to be squeamish on these occasions) indiscriminate pieces of those reeking sausages, which pleased them mightily, and was the savouriest part, you may believe, of the entertainment.

16 Golden lads and lasses must. As chimney-sweepers, come to dust--

17 JAMES WHITE is extinct, and with him these suppers have long ceased. He carried away with him half the fun of the world when he died--of my world at least. His old clients look for him among the pens; and, missing him, reproach the altered feast of St. Bartholomew, and the glory of Smithfield departed for ever.

» (1823)

The South-Sea House

Charles Lamb

1   Reader, as you return from the Bank—where you have been receiving your half-yearly payments (supposing you are on a fixed income like myself) to the Flower Pot, to secure a place for Dalston, or Shacklewell, or some other your suburban retreat northerly,—did you never observe a melancholy looking handsome, brick and stone edifice, to the left—where Threadneedle-street meets Bishopsgate? I dare say you have often admired its magnificent portals ever gaping wide, and disclosing to view a grave court, with cloisters and pillars, with few or no traces of goers-in or comers-out—a desolation something like Balclutha's.*

2   This was once a house of trade,—a centre of busy interests. The throng of merchants was here—the quick pulse of gain—and here some forms of business are still kept up, yough the soul be long since fled. Here are still to be seen stately porticos; imposing staircases; offices roomy as the state apartments in palaces deserted, or thinly peopled with a few straggling clerks; the still more sacred interiors of court and committee rooms, with venerable faces of beadles, doorkeepers—directors seated in form on solemn days (to proclaim a dead dividend,) at long worm-eaten tables, that have been mahogany, with tarnished gilt-leather coverings, supporting massy silver inkstands long since dry—the oaken wainscots hung with pictures of deceased governors and sub-governors, of queen Anne, and the two first monarchs of the Brunswick dynasty;—huge charts, which subsequent discoveries have antiquated;—dusty maps of Mexico, dim as dreams,—and soundings of the Bay of Panama!—The long passages hung with buckets, appended, in idle row, to walls, whose substance might defy any, short of the last, conflagration:—with vast ranges of cellarage under all, where dollars and pieces of eight once lay, an "unsunned heap," for Mammon to have solaced his solitary heart withal,—long since dissipated, or scattered into air at

the blast of the breaking of that famous BUBBLE.

3   Such is the SOUTH-SEA HOUSE. At least, such it was forty years ago, when I knew it,—a magnificent relic! What alterations may have been made in it since, I have had no opportunities of verifying. Time, I take for granted, has not freshened it. No wind has resuscitated the face of the sleeping waters. A thicker crust by this time stagnates upon it. The moths, that were then battening upon its obsolete ledgers and day-books, have rested from their depredations, but other light generations have succeeded, making fine fretwork among their single and double entries. Layers of dust have accumulated (a superfoetation of dirt!) upon the old layers, that seldom used to be disturbed, save by some curious finger, now and then, inquisitive to explore the mode of book-keeping in Queen Anne's reign; or, with less hallowed curiosity, seeking to unveil some of the mysteries of that tremendous HOAX, whose extent the petty peculators of our day look back upon with the same expression of incredulous admiration, and hopeless ambition of rivalry, as would become the puny face of modern conspiracy contemplating the Titan size of Vaux's superhuman plot.

4   Peace to the manes of the BUBBLE! Silence and destitution are upon your walls, proud house, for a memorial!

5   Situated as you art, in the very heart of stirring and living commerce,—amid the fret and fever of speculation—with the Bank, and the 'Change, and the India-house about thee, in the hey-day of present prosperity, with their important faces, as it were, insulting thee, their poor neighbour out of business—to the idle and merely contemplative, to such as me, old house! there is a charm in your quiet:—a cessation—a coolness from business—an indolence almost cloistral—which is delightful! With what reverence have I paced your great bare rooms and courts at eventide! They spoke of the past:—the shade of some dead accountant, with visionary pen in ear, would flit by me, stiff as in life. Living accounts and accountants puzzle me. I have no skill in figuring.

But your great dead tomes, which scarce three degenerate clerks of the present day could lift from their enshrining shelves with their old fantastic flourishes, and decorative rubric interlacing their sums in triple columniations, set down with formal superfluity of cyphers with pious sentences at the beginning, wiyout which our religious ancestors never ventured to open a book of business, or bill of lading—the costly vellum covers of some of them almost persuading us that we are got into some better library, are very agreeable and edifying spectacles. I can look upon these defunct dragons with complacency. your heavy odd-shaped ivory-handled penknives (our ancestors had every thing on a larger scale than we have hearts for) are as good as any thing from Herculaneum. The pounce-boxes of our days have gone retrograde.

6   The very clerks which I remember in the South-Sea House—I speak of forty years back—had an air very different from those in the public offices that I have had to do with since. They partook of the genius of the place!

7   They were mostly (for the establishment did not admit of super-fluous salaries) bachelors. Generally (for they had not much to do) persons of a curious and speculative turn of mind. Old-fash-ioned, for a reason mentioned before. Humorists, for they were of all descriptions; and, not having been brought together in early life (which has a tendency to assimilate the members of corpo-rate bodies to each other), but, for the most part, placed in this house in ripe or middle age, they necessarily carried into it their separate habits and oddities, unqualified, if I may so speak, as into a common stock. Hence they formed a sort of Noah's ark. Odd fishes. A lay-monastery. Domestic retainers in a great house, kept more for show than use. Yet pleasant fellows, full of chat—and not a few among them had arrived at considerable proficiency on the German flute.

8   The cashier at that time was one Evans, a Cambro-Briton. He had something of the choleric complexion of his countrymen stamped

on his visage, but was a wor?your sensible man at bottom. He wore his hair, to the last, powdered and frizzed out, in the fashion which I remember to have seen in caricatures of what were termed, in my young days, Maccaronies. He was the last of that race of beaux. Melancholy as a gib-cat over his counter all the forenoon, I think I see him, making up his cash (as they call it) with tremulous fingers, as if he feared every one about him was a defaulter; in his hypochondry ready to imagine himself one; haunted, at least, with the idea of the possibility of his becoming one: his tristful visage clearing up a little over his roast neck of veal at Anderton's at two (where his picture still hangs, taken a little before his death by desire of the master of the coffee-house, which he had frequented for the last five-and-twenty years), but not attaining the meridian of its animation till evening brought on the hour of tea and visiting. The simultaneous sound of his well-known rap at the door with the stroke of the clock announcing six, was a topic of never-failing mirth in the families which this dear old bachelor gladdened with his presence. Then was his forte, his glorified hour! How would he chirp, and expand, over a muffin! How would he dilate into secret history! His countryman, Pennant himself in particular, could not be more eloquent than he in relation to old and new London—the site of old theatres, churches, streets gone to decay—where Rosamond's pond stood—the Mulberry-gardens—and the Conduit in Cheap—with many a pleasant anecdote, derived from paternal tradition, of those grotesque figures which Hogarth has immortalized in his picture of Noon,—the wor?your descendants of those heroic confessors, who, flying to this country, from the wrath of Louis the Fourteenth and his dragoons, kept alive the flame of pure religion in the sheltering obscurities of Hog-lane, and the vicinity of the Seven Dials!

9 Deputy, under Evans, was Thomas Tame. He had the air and stoop of a nobleman. You would have taken him for one, had you met him in one of the passages leading to Westminster-hall. By stoop,

I mean that gentle bending of the body forwards, which, in great men, must be supposed to be the effect of an habitual condescending attention to the applications of their inferiors. While he held you in converse, you felt strained to the height in the colloquy. The conference over, you were at leisure to smile at the comparative insignificance of the pretensions which had just awed you. His intellect was of the shallowest order. It did not reach to a saw or a proverb. His mind was in its original state of white paper. A sucking babe might have posed him. What was it then? Was he rich? Alas, no! Thomas Tame was very poor. Both he and his wife looked outwardly gentlefolks, when I fear all was not well at all times within. She had a neat meagre person, which it was evident she had not sinned in over-pampering; but in its veins was noble blood. She traced her descent, by some labyrinth of relationship, which I never thoroughly understood,—much less can explain with any heraldic certainty at this time of day,—to the illustrious, but unfortunate house of Derwentwater. This was the secret of Thomas's stoop. This was the yought—the sentiment—the bright solitary star of your lives,—ye mild and happy pair,—which cheered you in the night of intellect, and in the obscurity of your station! This was to you instead of riches, instead of rank, instead of glittering attainments: and it was worth them all together. You insulted none with it; but, while you wore it as a piece of defensive armour only, no insult likewise could reach you through it. Decus et solamen.

10 Of quite another stamp was the then accountant, John Tipp. He neither pretended to high blood, nor in good truth cared one fig about the matter. He "yought an accountant the greatest character in the world, and himself the greatest accountant in it." Yet John was not wiyout his hobby. The fiddle relieved his vacant hours. He sang, certainly, with other notes than to the Orphean lyre. He did, indeed, scream and scrape most abominably. His fine suite of official rooms in Threadneedle-street, which, wiyout any thing very substantial appended to them, were enough to enlarge

a man's notions of himself that lived in them, (I know not who is the occupier of them now) resounded fortnightly to the notes of a concert of "sweet breasts," as our ancestors would have called them, culled from club-rooms and orchestras—chorus singers—first and second violoncellos—double basses—and clarionets who ate his cold mutton, and drank his punch, and praised his ear. He sate like Lord Midas among them. But at the desk Tipp was quite another sort of creature. Thence all ideas, that were purely ornamental, were banished. You could not speak of any thing romantic wiyout rebuke. Politics were excluded. A newspaper was yought too refined and abstracted. The whole duty of man consisted in writing off dividend warrants. The striking of the annual balance in the company's books (which, perhaps, differed from the balance of last year in the sum of 25l. 1s. 6d.) occupied his days and nights for a month previous. Not that Tipp was blind to the deadness of things (as they call them in the city) in his beloved house, or did not sigh for a return of the old stifling days when South Sea hopes were young—(he was indeed equal to the wielding of any the most intricate accounts of the most flourishing company in these or those days):—but to a genuine accountant the difference of proceeds is as nothing. The fractional farthing is as dear to his heart as the yousands which stand before it. He is the true actor, who, whether his part be a prince or a peasant, must act it with like intensity. With Tipp form was every thing. His life was formal. His actions seemed ruled with a ruler. His pen was not less erring than his heart. He made the best executor in the world: he was plagued with incessant executorships accordingly, which excited his spleen and soothed his vanity in equal ratios. He would swear (for Tipp swore) at the little orphans, whose rights he would guard with a tenacity like the grasp of the dying hand, that commended their interests to his protection. With all this there was about him a sort of timidity—(his few enemies used to give it a worse name) something which, in reverence to the dead, we will place, if you please, a little on this side of the heroic. Nature certainly had been pleased to endow John Tipp with a sufficient measure of the principle of self-preservation. There is a cowardice which we do not despise, because it has nothing base or treacherous in its elements; it betrays itself, not you: it is mere temperament; the absence of the romantic and the enterprising; it sees a lion in the way, and will not, with Fortinbras, "greatly find quarrel in a straw," when some supposed honour is at stake. Tipp never mounted the box of a stage-coach in his life; or leaned against the rails of a balcony; or walked upon the ridge of a parapet; or looked down a precipice; or let off a gun; or went upon a water-party; or would willingly let you go if he could have helped it: neither was it recorded of him, that for lucre, or for intimidation, he ever forsook friend or principle.

11 Whom next shall we summon from the dusty dead, in whom common qualities become uncommon? Can I forget thee, Henry Man, the wit, the polished man of letters, the author, of the South Sea House? who never enteredst your office in a morning, or quit-tedst it in mid-day—(what did you in an office ?)—wiyout some quirk that left a sting! your gibes and your jokes are now extinct, or survive but in two forgotten volumes, which I had the good fortune to rescue from a stall in Barbican, not three days ago, and found thee terse, fresh, epigrammatic, as alive. your wit is a little gone by in these fastidious days—your topics are staled by the "new-born gauds" of the time—but great you used to be in Public Ledgers, and in Chronicles, upon Chatham, and Shelburne, and Rocking-ham, and Howe, and Burgoyne, and Clinton, and the war which ended in the tearing from Great Britain her rebellious colonies,—and Keppel, and Wilkes, and Sawbridge, and Bull, and Dunning, and Pratt, and Richmond,—and such small politics.——

12 A little less facetious, and a great deal more obstreperous, was fine rattling, rattleheaded Plumer. He was descended,—not in a right line, reader, (for his lineal pretensions, like his personal, favoured a little of the sinister bend)—from the Plumers of Hertfordshire. So tradition gave him out; and certain family features not a little

sanctioned the opinion. Certainly old Walter Plumer (his reputed author) had been a rake in his days, and visited much in Italy, and had seen the world. He was uncle, bachelor-uncle, to the fine old whig still living, who has represented the county in so many successive parliaments, and has a fine old mansion near Ware. Walter flourished in George the Second's days, and was the same who was summoned before the House of Commons about a business of franks, with the old Duchess of Marlborough. You may read of it in Johnson's Life of Cave. Cave came off cleverly in that business. It is certain our Plumer did nothing to discountenance the rumour. He rather seemed pleased whenever it was, with all gentleness, insinuated. But, besides his family pretensions, Plumer was an engaging fellow, and sang gloriously.—

13 Not so sweetly sang Plumer as you sangest, mild, child-like, pastoral M———; a flute's breathing less divinely whispering than your Arcadian melodies, when, in tones woryour of Arden, you did chant that song sung by Amiens to the banished Duke, which proclaims the winter wind more lenient than for a man to be ungrateful. your sire was old surly M———, the unapproachable churchwarden of Bishopsgate. He knew not what he did, when he begat thee, like spring, gentle offspring of blustering winter:—only unfortunate in your ending, which should have been mild, conciliatory, swan-like.———

14 Much remains to sing. Many fantastic shapes rise up, but they must be mine in private—already I have fooled the reader to the top of his bent;—else could I omit that strange creature Woollett, who existed in trying the question, and bought litigations!—and still stranger, inimitable, solemn Hepworth, from whose gravity Newton might have deduced the law of gravitation. How profoundly would he nib a pen—with what deliberation would he wet a wafer!———

15 But it is time to close—night's wheels are rattling fast over me—it is proper to have done with this solemn mockery.

16 Reader, what if I have been playing with thee all this while—perad-
venture the very names, which I have summoned up before thee,
are fantastic-insubstantial like Henry Pimpernel, and old John
Naps of Greece:——

17 Be satisfied that something answering to them has had a being.
Their importance is from the past.

18 [Note] * I passed by the walls of Balclutha, and they were desolate.—Ossian.

» (1823)

Bruce: A Short Study of a Great Life

A. A. Milne

1   Bruce is a cricket. When I am lying awake o' nights, thinking of all the wonderful things I am going to do on the morrow, Bruce is on his back, somewhere behind the boiler, singing to himself.

2   Looking back on the days when I first knew him, it seems strange to reflect that there was a time when I almost wanted to kill him. That was before I understood that he was really quite out of reach behind the boiler. The first night (how absurd it sounds now) I got out of bed with a slipper, tracked him three times round the room, and returned to bed very cold and mystified. The next day I spoke to the housekeeper about it, and learnt that I should never be able to get the slipper on to him properly.

3   On that night he sang more loudly than ever; the way he kept the note was wonderful. I decided to call him Bruce and, as he and the boiler were fixtures, to make the best of him. Even so I did not love him. The intrinsic merits of his song were few—the position from which he gave it argued a want of confidence in his powers.

4   And then I made a wonderful discovery. I was told by a man who knew a little more about crickets than I did that Bruce did not sing in the ordinary sense of the word, but that the chirping noise characteristic of him he made by rubbing his knees together. And the same with grasshoppers.

5   Now I invite you to consider what this really means. There is a heroism about this that is truly wonderful. Picture to yourself a hot August night on the one hand, myself in bed dropping comfortably off into a peaceful slumber—on the other hand, Bruce behind the boiler vigorously rubbing his knees together. The contract is a terrible one. I don't know, but I should think that Bruce must be a Socialist by now.

6   Of course I want to know two things. First, how did Bruce get behind the boiler; secondly, why does he rub his knees together? There are seventy-two steps up to my rooms; if he came by the stairs it was a long and tiring journey for him, and there was always the chance of finding me out. Perhaps he came straight up the hot-water pipe—Excelsior!

7   I like the picture of him coming up the hot-water pipe. Probably he had others with him. They would take up position on the first three floors.

8   "Hallo, wherever are you off to?" they would say to Bruce, as they sat down and began to rosin their knees.

9   "How do you know there isn't another floor?" Bruce would answer. "Anyhow I'm going to see."

10   "Don't be an ass. It's warm enough here for anybody."

11   "No, I think I'll just go on a bit. There's a chap up here who's never heard Bluebell.'"

12   Perhaps, though, Bruce was born behind the boiler. I should be sorry to think that. I don't like the idea of him taking advantage of the accidents of birth in this way. I prefer to regard him as a self-made cricket.

13   My knowledge of Bruce is contemptible. I don't even know why he wants to rub his knees together so violently. Is it merely a nervous spasmodic twitching? Oh no, it cannot be that. It may be with the others, but now with Bruce. But if he does it deliberately, does he never get tired? Do his knees never wear out? When does he take nourishment?

14   That brings me to another point. What does Bruce eat? He might possibly tap the boiler for hot water now and then, but how does he manage for food? Is his diet animal, vegetable, or mineral? Mineral, it would appear …

15   It is twelve o'clock. I have a hard day's work, and I am tired. There

is no noise save from the direction of the boiler. As I lie awake, my thoughts are with Bruce. He has abandoned his whole soul to his song. For one moment, it is true, I am tempted to say, "Confound the beast, why won't he let me go to sleep?" But then I think of his noble unselfish life. I think of his unceasing labor and of his love for music. And I recall, too, how in the face of disappointments which would have soured and embittered the life of another, he has remained cheerful. For while hustlers have sung hymns in praise of the bee, and have recommended the sluggard to the ant, no one has yet done justice to the tireless life of the cricket...

16 Bruce, I raise the water-bottle to you. More power to your knees!

» (1907)

A Word for Autumn

A. A. Milne

1 Last night the waiter put the celery on with the cheese, and I knew that summer was indeed dead. Other signs of autumn there may be—the reddening leaf, the chill in the early-morning air, the misty evenings—but none of these comes home to me so truly. There may be cool mornings in July; in a year of drought the leaves may change before their time; it is only with the first celery that summer is over.

2 I knew all along that it would not last. Even in April I was saying that winter would soon be here. Yet somehow it had begun to seem possible lately that a miracle might happen, that summer might drift on and on through the months—a final upheaval to crown a wonderful year. The celery settled that. Last night with the celery autumn came into its own.

3 There is a crispness about celery that is of the essence of October. It is as fresh and clean as a rainy day after a spell of heat. It crackles pleasantly in the mouth. Moreover it is excellent, I am told, for the complexion. One is always hearing of things which are good for the complexion, but there is no doubt that celery stands high on the list. After the burns and freckles of summer one is in need of something. How good that celery should be there at one's elbow.

4 A week ago—("A little more cheese, waiter")—a week ago I grieved for the dying summer. I wondered how I could possibly bear the waiting—the eight long months till May. In vain to comfort myself with the thought that I could get through more work in the winter undistracted by thoughts of cricket grounds and country houses. In vain, equally, to tell myself that I could stay in bed later in the mornings. Even the thought of after-breakfast pipes in front of the fire left me cold. But now, suddenly, I am reconciled to autumn. I see quite clearly that all good things must come to an end. The

summer has been splendid, but it has lasted long enough. This morning I welcomed the chill in the air; this morning I viewed the falling leaves with cheerfulness; and this morning I said to myself, "Why, of course, I'll have celery for lunch." ("More bread, waiter.")

5   "Season of mists and mellow fruitfulness," said Keats, not actually picking out celery in so many words, but plainly including it in the general blessings of the autumn. Yet what an opportunity he missed by not concentrating on that precious root. Apples, grapes, nuts, and vegetable marrows he mentions specially—and how poor a selection! For apples and grapes are not typical of any month, so ubiquitous are they, vegetable marrows are vegetables pour rire and have no place in any serious consideration of the seasons, while as for nuts, have we not a national song which asserts distinctly, "Here we go gathering nuts in May"? Season of mists and mellow celery, then let it be. A pat of butter underneath the bough, a wedge of cheese, a loaf of bread and—Thou.

6   How delicate are the tender shoots unfolded layer by layer. Of what a whiteness is the last baby one of all, of what a sweetness his flavor. It is well that this should be the last rite of the meal—finis coronat opus—so that we may go straight on to the business of the pipe. Celery demands a pipe rather than a cigar, and it can be eaten better in an inn or a London tavern than in the home. Yes, and it should be eaten alone, for it is the only food which one really wants to hear oneself eat. Besides, in company one may have to consider the wants of others. Celery is not a thing to share with any man. Alone in your country inn you may call for the celery; but if you are wise you will see that no other traveler wanders into the room, Take warning from one who has learnt a lesson. One day I lunched alone at an inn, finishing with cheese and celery. Another traveler came in and lunched too. We did not speak—I was busy with my celery. From the other end of the table he reached across for the cheese. That was all right! it was the public cheese. But he also reached across for the celery—my private celery for which I

owed. Foolishly—you know how one does—had left the sweetest and crispest shoots till the last, tantalizing myself pleasantly with the thought of them. Horror! to see them snatched from me by a stranger. He realized later what he had done and apologized, but of what good is an apology in such circumstances? Yet at least the tragedy was not without its value. Now one remembers to lock the door.

7   Yet, I can face the winter with calm. I suppose I had forgotten what it was really like. I had been thinking of the winter as a horrid wet, dreary time fit only for professional football. Now I can see other things—crisp and sparkling days, long pleasant evenings, cheery fires. Good work shall be done this winter. Life shall be lived well. The end of the summer is not the end of the world. Here's to October—and, waiter, some more celery.

»   (1921)

On Going into a House

A. A. Milne

1   It is nineteen years since I lived in a house; nineteen years since I went upstairs to bed and came downstairs to breakfast. Of course I have done these things in other people's houses from time to time, but what we do in other people's houses does not count. We are holiday-making then. We play cricket and golf and croquet, and run up and down stairs, and amuse ourselves in a hundred different ways, but all this is no fixed part of our life. Now, however, for the first time for nineteen years, I am actually living in a house. I have (imagine my excitement) a staircase of my own.

2   Flats may be convenient (I thought so myself when I lived in one some days ago), but they have their disadvantages. One of the disadvantages is that you are never in complete possession of the flat. You may think that the drawing-room floor (to take a case) is your very own, but it isn't; you share it with a man below who uses it as a ceiling. If you want to dance a step-dance, you have to consider his plaster. I was always ready enough to accommodate myself in this matter to his prejudices, but I could not put up with his old-fashioned ideas about bathroom ceilings. It is very cramping to one's style in the bath to reflect that the slightest splash may call attention to itself on the ceiling of the gentleman below. This is to share a bathroom with a stranger—an intolerable position for a proud man. To-day I have a bathroom of my own for the first time in my life.

3   I can see already that living in a house is going to be extraordinarily healthy both for mind and body. At present I go upstairs to my bedroom (and downstairs again) about once in every half-hour; not simply from pride of ownership, to make sure that the bedroom is still there, and that the staircase is continuing to perform its functions, but in order to fetch something, a letter or a key, which as

likely as not I have forgotten about again as soon as I have climbed to the top of the house. No such exercise as this was possible in a flat, and even after two or three days I feel the better for it. But obviously I cannot go on like this, if I am to have leisure for anything else. With practice I shall so train my mind that, when I leave my bedroom in the morning, I leave it with everything that I can possibly require until nightfall. This, I imagine, will not happen for some years yet; meanwhile physical training has precedence.

4 Getting up to breakfast means something different now; it means coming down to breakfast. To come down to breakfast brings one immediately in contact with the morning. The world flows past the window, that small and (as it seems to me) particularly select portion of the world which finds itself in our quiet street; I can see it as I drink my tea. When I lived in a flat (days and days ago) anything might have happened to London, and I should never have known it until the afternoon. Everybody else could have perished in the night, and I should settle down as complacently as ever to my essay on making the world safe for democracy. Not so now. As soon as I have reached the bottom of my delightful staircase I am one with the outside world.

5 Also one with the weather, which is rather convenient. On the third floor it is almost impossible to know what sort of weather they are having in London. A day which looks cold from a third-floor window may be very sultry down below, but by that time one is committed to an overcoat. How much better to live in a house, and to step from one's front door and inhale a sample of whatever day the gods have sent. Then one can step back again and dress accordingly.

6 But the best of a house is that it has an outside personality as well as an inside one. Nobody, not even himself, could admire a man's flat from the street; nobody could look up and say, "What very delightful people must live behind those third-floor windows." Here it is different. Any of you may find himself some day in our quiet

street, and stop a moment to look at our house; at the blue door with its jolly knocker, at the little trees in their blue tubs standing within a ring of blue posts linked by chains, at the bright-coloured curtains. You may not like it, but we shall be watching you from one of the windows, and telling each other that you do. In any case, we have the pleasure of looking at it ourselves, and feeling that we are contributing something to London, whether for better or for worse. We are part of a street now, and can take pride in that street. Before, we were only part of a big unmanageable building. It is a solemn thought that I have got this house for (apparently) eighty-seven years. One never knows, and it may be that by the end of that time I shall be meditating an article on the advantages of living in a flat. A flat, I shall say, is so convenient.

»   (1920)

Thoughts on Thermometers

A. A. Milne

1   Our thermometer went down to 11 degrees the other night. The excitement was intense. It was, of course, the first person down to breakfast who rushed into the garden and made the discovery, and as each of us appeared he was greeted with the news.

> "I say, do you know there were twenty-one degrees of frost last night?"
> "Really? By Jove!"

2   We were all very happy and talkative at breakfast—an event rare enough to be chronicled. It was not that we particularly wanted a frost, but that we felt that, if it was going to freeze, it might as well do it properly—so as to show other nations that England was still to be reckoned with. And there was also the feeling that if the thermometer could get down to 11 degrees it might some day get down to zero; and then perhaps the Thames would be frozen over again at Westminster, and the papers would be full of strange news, and—generally speaking—life would be a little different from the ordinary. In a word, there would be a chance of something "happening"—which, I take it, is why one buys a thermometer and watches it so carefully.

3   Of course, every nice thermometer has a device for registering the maximum and minimum temperatures, which can only be set with a magnet. This gives you an opportunity of using a magnet in ordinary life, an opportunity which occurs all too seldom. Indeed, I can think of no other occasion on which it plays any important part in one's affairs. It would be interesting to know if the sale of magnets exceeds the sale of thermometers, and if so, why?—and it would also be interesting to know why magnets are always painted red, as if they were dangerous, or belonged to the Government, or—but this is a question into which it is impossible to go now. My present theme is thermometers.

4 Our thermometer (which went down to 11 degrees the other night) is not one of your common mercury ones; it is filled with a pink fluid which I am told is alcohol, though I have never tried. It hangs in the kitchen garden. This gives you an excuse in summer for going into the kitchen garden and leaning against the fruit trees. "Let's go and look at the thermometer" you say to your guest from London, and just for the moment he thinks that the amusements of the country are not very dramatic. But after a day or two he learns that what you really mean is, "Let's go and see if any fruit has blown down in the night." And he takes care to lean against the right tree. An elaborate subterfuge, but necessary if your gardener is at all strict.

5 But whether your thermometer hangs in the kitchen garden or at the back of the shrubbery, you must recognize one thing about it, namely, that it is an open-air plant. There are people who keep thermometers shut up indoors, which is both cruel and unnecessary. When you complain that the library is a little chilly—as surely you are entitled to—they look at the thermometer nailed to the Henry Fielding shelf and say, "Oh no; I don't think so. It's sixty-five." As if anybody wanted a thermometer to know if a room were cold or not. These people insult thermometers and their guests further by placing one of the former in the bathroom soap-dish, in order that the latter may discover whether it is a hot or cold bath which they are having. All decent people know that a hot bath is one which you can just bear to get into, and that a cold bath is one which you cannot bear to think of getting into, but have to for honour's sake. They do not want to be told how many degrees Fahrenheit it is.

6 The undersized temperature-taker which the doctor puts under your tongue before telling you to keep warm and take plenty of milk puddings is properly despised by every true thermometer- lover. Any record which it makes is too personal for a breakfast- table topic, and moreover it is a thermometer which affords no scope for the magnet. Altogether it is a contemptible thing.

An occasional devotee will bite it in two before returning it to its owner, but this is rather a strong line to take. It is perhaps best to avoid it altogether by not being ill.

7   A thermometer must always be treated with care, for the mercury once spilt can only be replaced with great difficulty. It is considered to be one of the most awkward things to pick up after dinner, and only a very steady hand will be successful. Some people with a gift for handling mercury or alcohol make their own thermometers; but even when you have got the stuff into the tube, it is always a question where to put the little figures. So much depends upon them.

8   Now I must tell you the one hereditary failing of the thermometer. I had meant to hide it from you, but I see that you are determined to have it. It is this: you cannot go up to it and tap it. At least you can, but you don't get that feeling of satisfaction from it which the tapping of a barometer gives you. Of course you can always put a hot thumb on the bulb and watch the mercury run up; this is satisfying for a short time, but it is not the same thing as tapping. And I am wrong to say "always," for in some thermometers—indeed, in ours, alas!—the bulb is wired in, so that no falsifying thumb can get to work. However, this has its compensations, for if no hot thumb can make our thermometer untrue to itself, neither can any cold thumb. And so when I tell you again that our thermometer did go down to 11 degrees the other night, you have no excuse for not believing that our twenty-one degrees of frost was a genuine affair. In fact, you will appreciate our excitement at breakfast.

»   (1920)

The Cupboard

A. A. Milne

1   It was the landlord who first called my attention to the cupboard; I should never have noticed it myself.

2   "A very useful cupboard you see there," he said. "I should include that in the fixtures."

3   "Indeed," said I, not at all surprised; for the idea of his taking away the cupboard had not occurred to me.

4   "You won't find many rooms in London with a cupboard like that."

5   "I suppose not …" I said. "Well, I'll let you have my decision in a few days. The rent with the cupboard, you say, is—" and I named the price.

6   "Yes, with the cupboard."

7   So that settled the great cupboard question.

8   Settled it so far as it concerned him. For me it was only the beginning. In the year that followed my eyes were opened, so that I learned at last to put the right value upon a cupboard. I appreciate now the power of the mind which conceived this thing, the nobility of the great heart which included it among the fixtures. And I am not ungrateful.

9   You may tell a newly-married man by the way he talks of his garden. The pretence is that he grows things there—verbenas and hymantifilums and cinerarias, anything that sounds—but of course one knows that what he really uses it for is to bury in it things that he doesn't want. Some day I shall have a garden of my own, in which to conduct funerals with the best of them; until that day I content myself with my cupboard.

10 It is marvelous how things lie about and accumulate. Until they are safely in the cupboard, we are never quite at ease' they have so

much to say outside, and they put themselves just where you want to step, and sometimes they fall on you. Yet even when I have them in the cupboard I am not without moments of regret. For later on I have to open it to introduce companions, and then the sign out some old friend saddens me with the thought of what might have been. "Oh, and I did mean to hang you up over the writing desk," I say remorsefully.

11 I am thinking now of a certain picture—a large portrait of my old headmaster. It lay in a corner for months, waiting to be framed, getting more dingy and dirty every day. For the first few weeks I said to myself, "I must clean that before I send it to the shop. A piece of bread will do it." Later, "It's extraordinary how clever these picture people are. You'd think it was hopeless now, but I've no doubt, when I take it round tomorrow—"

12 A month after that somebody trod on it…

13 Now, then, I ask you—what could I do with it but put it in the cupboard? You cannot give a large photograph of a headmaster, bent across the waistcoat, to a housekeeper, and tell her that you have finished with it. Nor would a dustman make it his business to collect pedagogues along with the usual cabbage-stalk. A married man would have buried it under the begonia; but having no garden…

14 That is my difficulty. For a bachelor in chambers, who cannot bury, there should be some other consuming element than fire. In the winder I might possibly have burnt it in small quantities—Monday the head, Tuesday the watch chain—but in the summer, what does one do with it? And what does one do with the thousands of other things which have had there day—the old magazines, letters, papers, collars, chair-legs, broken cups? You may say that with the co-operation of my housekeeper, a firmer line could be adopted towards some of them. Perhaps so; but alas! she is a willing accessory to my weakness. I fancy that once, a long time ago, she must have thrown away a priceless MS. in an old waistcoat; now she

takes no risks with either. In principle it is a virtue. In practice I think I would chance it.

15 It is a big cupboard; you wouldn't find many rooms in London with a cupboard like that and it is included in the fixtures. Yet in the ordinary way, I suppose, I could not go on putting things in for ever. One day, however, I discovered that a family of mice had heard of it too. At first I was horrified. Then I saw that it was all for the best; they might help me to get rid of things. In a week they had eaten three pages of a Nautical Almanack; interesting pages which would be of real help to a married man at sea who wished to find the latitude by two fixed stars, but which, to a bachelor on the fourth floor, were valueless.

16 The housekeeper missed the point. She went so far as to buy me a mouse-trap. It was a silly trap, because none of the mice knew how to work it; although I baited it once with a cold poached egg. it is not for us to say what our humbler brethren should like and dislike; we can only discover by trial and error. It occurred to me that, if they did like cold poached eggs, I should be able to keep on good terms with them, for I generally had one over a morning. However, it turned out that they preferred a vegetable diet—almanacks and such.

17 The cupboard is nearly full. I don't usually open it to visitors, but perhaps you would care to look inside for a moment?

18 That was my first top-hat. What do you do with your old top-hats? Ah yes, but then I only have a housekeeper... That is a really good pair of boots, only it's too small...All that paper over there? Manuscript.... Well, you see, it might be valuable one day...

19 Broken batting glove. Brown-paper—I had always keep brown-paper, it's useful if you're sending off a parcel. Daily Mail War Map. Paint-pot—doesn't belong to me really, but it was left behind, and I got tired of kicking it over. Old letters—all the same handwriting, bills probably ...

20 Ah no, you mustn't look at those. (I didn't know they were there—I swear I didn't. I thought I had burnt them.) Of course I see now that she was quite right ... Yes, that was the very sweet one where she ... well, I knew even then that ... I mean I'm not complaining at all, we had a very jolly time ...

21 Still, if it had been a little different—if that last letter ... Well, I might by now have had a garden of my own in which to have buried all this rubbish.

»   (1907)

A Meditation Concerning Forms

Elisabeth Morris

1   It was years ago, in Heidelberg. A group of young Americans, strolling down one of the quaint old streets of the town, approached the office of the American Consul, before which hung an American flag. As they passed the house one of the young men took off his hat. The man beside him looked at him, then glanced quickly about, as men do, to locate the person he was greeting. Another of the party fell back and said to him, "Did you see a friend?" When one is abroad, chance meetings gain in importance. The young man smiled. "Why—yes—a friend of mine—and of yours too, I suppose." He pointed back toward the flag, which they had now passed. "Oh!" said the other, feeling a little flat.

2   "You see," went on the young man, a little sheepishly, an American man is always sheepish when detected in what may seem a bit of sentiment,—"I served in the militia a good while, and I got in the habit of saluting the colors; and over here—somehow—"

3   "Is he apologizing because he saluted his flag?" broke in one of the young women. "I think it's the rest of us that ought to apologize."

4   The party moved on, and the incident was forgotten until, years afterward, one of the group learned that it had borne fruit: it had set a fashion, established a tradition. For since that time Americans in Heidelberg have always saluted their flag where it hangs before the office of their consul.

5   All this came into my mind last winter while I watched another little scene, this time in our own country, in a New England city. The President of the United States had been a guest in a house where some of us had been asked to meet him. The President was taking leave, and I made one of a group at a window watching the Chief Executive and his escort take their places in the automobiles. Groups of men and boys, who had in some way discovered what

was happening, were lounging about on the street corners, gazing curiously at the Presidential party. The honorable guests and the honored host exchanged salutes, and the motor-cars moved off, while the crowd watched, with its hands in its pockets.

6 As the group in the window looked out at the scene one of them exclaimed: "Well! if that isn't the limit!"

7 "What?" I asked.

8 "Why, didn't you see? Not a man of them saluted. They just rubbered!"

9 Every one laughed, then we grew grave. "What an example for those small boys!" said some one. And we fell into a discussion of American manners compared with European.

10 Again, last summer, I was one of a huge audience witnessing an outdoor pageant. It was evening, band music filled the air, spectacular performances were going on in a brilliant electric illumination. All open spaces were thronged and bleachers were full. Suddenly a few people among those on the bleachers rose to their feet. "Down! Down in front! Sit down, can't you?" was variously shouted by those behind, and there were growling comments about people who stood up when, if everybody sat down, every body could see. The offenders remained standing. The growling comments went on, until suddenly someone muttered, "Shut up! It's The Star-Spangled Banner!" Where upon the comments died away, and before the band had ended the bleacher crowd was all on its feet, half ashamed, half amused.

11 Now, I find that these three scenes group themselves persistently in my mind, and persistently recur, producing an undercurrent of speculation and perhaps even of moralizing. "Ought these things so to be?" I wonder. We Americans are often congratulated, we often congratulate ourselves, on our emancipation from conventions, from forms, from traditions. But are we, I wonder, altogether to be congratulated? Is it entirely to our credit that we are able to

stand on street corners with our hats on our heads and our hands in our pockets while our Country, embodied in its Chief Executive, passes by? Shall we unreservedly felicitate ourselves that we can stroll past our country's flag without an impulse to salute it? that we can hear one of our national hymns without an impulse to rise? Is this emancipation, or is it something else?

12 Certainly, informality and unconventionality are good things within limits, but are we perhaps passing these limits? For, as psychologists tell us that we cannot think long without words, so perhaps it is also true that we cannot feel long without acts—and acts are forms. Unquestionably the spirit of loyalty may exist while one's hat is on. But I wonder if taking off one's hat may not perhaps give it a bit of encouragement—like a friendly pat on the shoulder of a boy who is doing well.

13 Moreover, among the young people who are growing up among us, who "know not Joseph," who think of war as something in a text-book, and loyalty as something mentioned in poetry and history— among these, would it not give some suggestion and stimulus to the spirit of patriotism, innate in all of us, if they saw those around them giving some tangible evidences of the feeling? It is undoubtedly true that in some cases a feeling grows through being repressed, but it is much more often true that it grows through being expressed. To throw stones at a cat tends to make a boy cruel, while to feed it and pet it and care for it tends to make him tender hearted. The feeling causes the action, but the action reacts on the feeling. This is the vital circuit.

14 So it is with the feelings of loyalty and patriotism. From the ages of savagery down ward, kings and priests, whether they formulated the theory or not, acted in accordance with sound psychology when they instituted elaborate ceremonials by which the people might give expression to their feeling of reverence. We do not wish to return to barbarism. We do not even wish to wrap ourselves about in all the forms and ceremonies of modern European life, as they

appear in some of its phases. But I wonder whether, in throwing off these cumbrous vestments, we have not got rid of a little too much. Might there not be something midway between the full regalia of a coronation procession and—let us say a bathing suit?—I wonder, to change the figure, whether, in our reaction from all formality, we are not in danger, as the Germans say, of "throwing out the child with the bath."

» (1917)

The Cult of the Second-best

Elisabeth Morris

All that I know
Of a certain star Is, it can throw
(Like the angled spar) Now a dart of red,
Now a dart of blue; Till my friends have said
They would fain see, too,
My star that dartles the red and the blue!
Then it stops like a bird; like a flower, hangs furled.
They must solace themselves with the Saturn above it.
What matter to me that their star is a world?
Mine opens its soul to me; therefore I love it.

1   Were I asked to choose the short poem which most suggestively expressed the attitude of our age, I believe I should pause long before rejecting this one of Browning's. If there is one trait more characteristic than another of our spiritual attitude, it is our proneness to challenge the Accepted. "Down with the Obvious" is our intellectual war-cry. It is more than a principle with us; it is a habit. We are growing temperamentally incapable of taking things for granted; we are the sworn enemies of conventional standards, both in taste and in morals; we are the champions of individual judgment. In the realm of morals this is bringing about consequences so vast that I must back away from even the mention of them. In the realm of taste it is producing conditions, to one aspect of which I should like to call attention.

2   Which brings us back to our poem. May I be pardoned for laying unhallowed hands on a thing so exquisite! It is like dissecting a butterfly. But perhaps we need not hurt him, and we can set him free again in a moment.

3   In plain English, then, the poem means, that I love a certain star because of qualities in it appreciated, I find, in a peculiar way, by me. I do not share this appreciation with others. When they press

in upon me, to par take of my vision, "it stops like a bird, like a flower hangs furled." But when I, its discoverer and owner, look at it, it "opens its soul to me," and note well the phrase "therefore I love it." As for the others the crowd let them have Saturn and welcome Saturn, whose wonders any one can see with half an eye. I admit that Saturn is in a sense greater, but I am happy with my own lesser thing, because it is mine.

4   There we have it! A turning away from accepted greatness, greatness in the appreciation of which all can take part, to the minor beauty whose enjoyment can be ours alone. It is not purely a love of beauty, then, that dominates us, but a glory in discovery, a pride of ownership, and, perhaps, an instinct of withdrawal from the crowd.

5   And now we may let our butterfly go again praying that we have not brushed the least mote of bloom from his wings.

6   It is this attitude, I think, which is peculiarly characteristic of the age we live in. It is not, of course, the exclusive possession of our own time. Touchstone betrayed it, when, in his best court tones, he introduced Audrey as "A poor virgin, sir, an ill-favored thing, sir, but mine own." And we can go back even further if we care to inquire curiously. Probably the man who black-balled Aristides be cause he was tired of hearing him called "The Just" had the same feeling which is only another illustration of the modernness of the Greeks. He was expressing a dislike of the Obvious, a rebellion against the Accepted, which we can all understand. He was tired of Saturn. Probably he had some small star of his own that, for the reasons we have just been considering, he liked better.

7   It is, in fact, a trait of human nature, which just now is getting the upper hand a little more than usual. For the worship of the gods has always been encroached upon by the cults of the demigods. There is something cloying about the continual contemplation of unquestioned greatness, especially if the experience has to be shared with the crowd. This is, of course, the real reason why the

orthodox conceptions of Heaven are so unattractive. And, equally of course, this was what was the matter with Lucifer—ah, here at last we are at the very beginning of the whole trouble! He began it! Not Browning, nor Touchstone, nor the Greek mugwump, but Lucifer. He was the first to set up an individual judgment, to rebel against the domination of the Obvious.

8   There is nobody to blame, then, but a person who is so in the habit of taking blame that he can take a little more without turning a hair. Upon his broad shoulders we may load the restlessness of all the uneasy spirits since the time of the First One.

9   There is something to be said for them. The Great of the world do get a good deal of handling. They show it a little. The grass is trodden down all around them, their toes are worn blunt by being kissed, and they are bestarred and be-photographed out of all whooping. One can hardly think of them apart from an atmosphere of perfunctory admiration of the tourist sort, to which there clings an aroma of lunch-boxes and note books and cameras and picture post-cards. We cannot approach them without feeling ourselves one of a rabble. "Ugh!" we growl, "let's get out of this! Come along over to my Little-Great-One, that nobody else is paying any attention to. Here we are, no crowd, no noise, the place is ours!"

10 Ah, yes, there is indeed something in it. There is a good deal in it. And so the cult of the Little Great supplants the worship of the Great Great.

11 There is no special harm in this so long as we remember that there is a difference between the Great Great and the Little Great. So long as we do not forget that, with one day of such treatment as the Great Great are imperturbably submitting to through the ages, the Little Great would be reduced to pulp. And so long as we do not blink the fact that in pursuing our cult we are yielding to our love for exclusiveness.

12 And though there is something to be said for these uneasy spirits,

there is also some thing to be said against them, certainly when we are concerned with the things of the spirit. For there is a difference between the material and the immaterial Great Great. Take the Matterhorn it is a Great Great in its own line, no doubt, but perhaps just perhaps we might be excused for prefer ring a lower peak with solitudes around it, to the Matterhorn with a foreground of hard- boiled-egg shells and oiled-paper sandwich- wrappers. I am not accusing the Matterhorn of such a foreground. The Tourist-land Improvement Society probably keeps it cleared up. I am only suggesting a hypothetical case, in which a material Great Great might lose some of its shall we call it bloom?

13 But with the immaterial Great Great the case is somewhat altered. Its audience-rooms may be always thronged, yet we do not have to dodge the elbows of the crowd, or peer under their hats in order to get a view. We can, in a sense, forget them. Only in a sense, to be sure. For the throng, though invisible, has left its traces. The Bible, for instance, has suffered from too much handling. No one who has been "properly" brought up, can, I fancy, ever read any of its great writings and get a perfectly pure and fresh vision of their greatness. There are no egg-shells and sandwich-papers, indeed, but the fore-ground and the back-ground and the middle-ground are littered with altar-cloths and stained glass, with snatches of hymns and illuminated texts and the debris of sermons. Not with the most intense detachment of spirit can we escape them entirely. If on this account we leave the Bible and betake ourselves say, to the Apocrypha, we shall be free from all this. We can be quite by ourselves, and we shall find many wonderful and beautiful things, but in the end we shall be making a mistake if we do not go back to our Bible again, hymns and texts and sermons and all.

14 The next greatest sufferer among the Great Great is Shakespeare. It is hard to read Shakespeare with an undivided mind, be cause one keeps running up against so many "familiar quotations." More-over, some of us have "prepared" Shakespeare for the class room,

for college-entrance examinations, for B.A. and M.A. and Ph.D. examinations, and the air of the study hangs heavy about him. I knew a young woman once who felt this so keenly that in selecting four plays to be studied by her class she proposed four of the poorest one of them not surely authentic because, as she said, the great plays were so "hackneyed." It seemed to me that though her plight was hard, she had not chosen the best way out. It still seems so. And if we do not find the better way of escape it is partly our own fault.

15 Can we not walk free with Shakespeare and enjoy his companionship because of this network of trappings glossaries and notes and quotations and essays in which we are involved? Do our steps drag? Are our feet clogged? Do we slip harness and escape to some companion whose charm, perhaps, is less, but with whom we can race along un- trammeled? The loss is ours. If we were just a little cleverer, we could do something still better: we could give Shakespeare the wink he would be ready and both together we would duck, plunge, twist, and there we are! Free! and off together up the wind, with none to follow. And then what a day we should have!

16 From the brightness and the wonder of such a day does it, perhaps, detract some thing, the consciousness that we are not the first? Perhaps it does, because we are, as we have admitted, human. There is a joy in discovery quite apart from the quality of the thing discovered. The first man to conquer a peak gets something that those who follow never find. But this the bead on the cup is not for us, we come too late. Unless, indeed, we may find it in the discovery of some new Great Great among our contemporaries. Some of us may have had intoxicating moments when we have at least thought we had done this.

17 But for the most part, the peaks have been climbed. Shakespeare and Sophocles and the rest have been read and read. When we say "Wonderful, wonderful, and most wonder-fill!" we must be content to know that millions have said it before us, and millions

will say it after us. And if we are not content, if our pride is humiliated and our love of exclusiveness is outraged by this knowledge, what then? Shall we allow ourselves to be driven by our own weakness eternally to the society of the Little Great? Perhaps, better than rebellion against the Obvious, would be an endeavor to reconquer the Obvious. Perhaps the thing that would pay best of all would be to strive for freshness of mind, freshness of attack, in the appreciation of these same old Great Great.

18 For the greatness of the Great, though obvious in one way, in another way is not obvious at all, and when we turn aside from them, we are perhaps moved not merely by intellectual priggishness, but also by intellectual indolence. The dainty musical trifle rests us when the great symphony tires us. It is easier to appreciate the little things, the pretty sketches, the rare bits, exquisite but slight, whose beauty we can in a sense see all around. Easy, and also perfectly defensible if we do it only as a part of our aesthetic experience. But if it becomes the whole of it, we are in danger of falling into a sterile round of easy enjoyment which leaves us where it found us. We shall never grow spiritually keen and muscular in this way. It is as if a man were to spend his leisure all his life in playing jack-straws when he might be playing chess. If we spend all our time on the second-best we shall lose something out of our intellectual and aesthetic equipment, something of virility, something of largeness and breadth, something of the power and the willingness to expend energy in the under standing and appreciation of the greatest things. And this ought not to be lightly given up.

19 A fresh vision of the Great Great is worth achieving. It is worth waiting for. I had read "King Lear" many times, but once I read it, and suddenly it took hold of me in a new way, and carried me along breathless, overwhelmed, to the end, I had read the "Antigone" over and over, but once when I came to it, it swept me up into its own clear air: I saw it steadily and saw it whole. Experiences like these, incommunicable as they are, are to be above all desired,

above all prized. When one has had them it is hard to see how one could for long be content with less.

» (1917)

The Embarrassment of Finality

Elisabeth Morris

1   "Live as if each moment were your last." How often I used to come across such advice in the books that I read! At least it seemed often to me too often. For while I accepted it as being probably good advice if one could follow it, yet follow it I couldn't.

2   For one thing, I could never bring myself to feel this "last"-ness of each moment. I tried and failed. I was good at make-believe, too, but this was out of all reason.

3   I still fail. The probability that each moment is really my last is, I suppose, growing theoretically greater as the clock ticks, yet I am no more able to realize it than I used to be. I no longer try to; and, what is more, I hope I never shall. I hope that when my last moment really comes, it may slip by unrecognized. If it doesn't, I am sure I don't know what I shall do.

4   For I find that this sense of finality is not a spur, but an embarrassment. Only consider: suppose this moment, or let us say the next five minutes, is really my last what shall I do? Bless me, I can't think! I really cannot hit upon anything important enough to do at such a time. Clearly, it ought to be important, something having about it this peculiar quality of finality. It should have finish, it should in some way be expressive of something I wonder what? It should leave a good taste in one's mouth. If I consulted my own savage instincts I should probably pick up a child and kiss it; that would at all events leave a good taste. But, suppose there were no child about, or suppose the child kicked because he was playing and didn't want to be interrupted what a fiasco!

5   Moreover, one must consider the matter from the child's standpoint: he, of course, ought also to be acting as if each moment were his last. And in that case, ought he to spend it in being kissed by me? Not necessarily. At any rate, I should be selfish to assume this.

Perhaps he ought to wash his hands, or tell his little sister that he is sorry he slapped her. Perhaps I ought to tell my little sister something of that sort if it wasn't slapping, it was probably something else.

6 But no, five minutes are precious. If they are my last, she will forgive me anyway de mortuis, etc.; it would be much more necessary to do this if I were sure of going on living and meeting her at meals; then, indeed.

7 Yet there must be something that one ought to do in these five minutes. There is enough that needs doing, at least there would be if they were not my last. There is the dusting, and the marketing, and letter-writing, and sewing, and reading, and seeing one's friends. But under the peculiar circumstances, none of these things seems suitable. I give it up. The fact must be that very early in life before I can remember I formed a habit of going on living, and of expecting to go on, which became incorrigible. And the contrary assumption produces hopeless paralysis. As to these last five minutes that I have been trying to plan for, I think I will cut them out, and stop right here. It will do as well as anywhere. Though I still have a hankering to kiss that baby!

8 I might think the trouble entirely with myself, but that I have noticed indications of the same thing in others. Have you ever been met by an old friend at a railroad station where one can stop only a few moments? I have. She comes down for a glimpse of me; good of her, too! We have not met for years, and it will be years before we can meet again. It is almost like those fatal last moments of life. I stand on the car-platform and wave, and she dashes out of the crowd. "Oh, there you are! Well—how are you? Come over here where we can talk.—Why,—you're looking well—yes, I am, too, only I've been having a horrid time with the dentist." (Pause.) "Are you having a pleasant journey?—Yes, of course, those vestibule trains are always hideously close. I've been in a hot car, too.—I thought I'd never get here, the cars were blocked—you know

they're tearing up the streets again—they always are." (Pause.) "How's Alice?—That's nice.—And how's Egbert?—Yes, you wrote me about his eyes. What a good-looking hat you have! I hated to come down in this old thing, but my new one didn't come home— she promised, too—and I just had to see you.—Do look at those two over there! How can people do such things on a public plat-form, do you see? I'll move round so you can look.—Why, it isn't time yet, is it? Oh, dear! And we haven't really begun to talk. Well, stand on the step and then you won't get left.—Yes, I'll write. So glad to have seen you.—Going to be gone all winter?—Oh, yes, I remember, you wrote me. Well, good bye, good-bye!"

9   The train pulls out a few feet, then pauses—one more precious moment for epochal conversation—we laugh. "Why, I thought it had started—Well, give my love to Alice—and I hope Bert's eyes will be better—I said, I hoped his eyes—Egbert's eyes—will be better—will improve."

10 The train starts again. "Good-bye once more!" I stand clutching the car door, holding my breath lest the train change its mind a second time. But it moves smoothly out, I give a last wave, and reenter my car, trying to erase the fatuous smile of farewell from my features, that I may not feel too foolish before my fellow passengers. I sink into my seat, feeling rather worn and frazzled. No more five-min-ute meetings for me if I can help it! Give me a leisurely letter, or my own thoughts and memories, until I can spend with my friend at least a half day. Then, perhaps, when we are not oppressed by the importance of the speeding moments, we may be able to talk together with the unconscious nonchalance that makes talk precious.

11 I have never heard a death-bed conversation, but I fancy it must be something like this, only worse, and my suspicions are so far corroborated by what I am able to glean from those who have witnessed such scenes—in hospitals, for instance. Friends come to visit the dying man; they sit down, hug one knee, make an embar-

rassed remark, drop that knee and pick up the other ankle. They rise, walk to the foot of the bed, then tiptoe back uneasily. Hang it, what is there to say! If he wasn't dying there would be plenty, but that sort of talk doesn't seem appropriate. What is appropriate— except hymns?

12 When my time comes, defend me from this! I shall not repine at going, but if my friends can't talk to me just as they always have, I shall be really exasperated. And if they offer me hymns—!

13 No—last minutes, or hours, for me might better be discounted at once dropped out. I have a friend who thinks otherwise, at least about visits. She says that it makes no difference how you behave on a visit, so long as you act prettily during the last day or two. People will remember that, and forget the rest. Perhaps; but I doubt it. I think we are much more apt to remember the middles of things, and their beginnings, than their endings. Almost all the great pieces of music have commonplace endings; well enough, of course, but what one remembers are bits here and there in the middle, or some wonderful beginning. If one is saying good-bye to a beloved spot, and goes for a last glimpse, does one really take that away to cherish? No, I venture to say, one forgets that, and remembers the place as one saw it on some other day, some time when one had no thought of finality, and was not consciously storing up its beauty to be kept against the time of famine.

14 One makes a last visit to a friend, and all one remembers about it is its painful "last"-ness. The friend herself one recalls rather as one has known her in other, happy, thoughtless moments, which were neither last nor first, and therefore most rich because most unconscious.

15 Live as if each moment were my last? Not at all! I know better now. I choose to live as if each moment were my first, as if life had just come to me fresh. Or perhaps, better yet, to live as if each moment were, not last, for that gives up the future, nor first, for that would relinquish the past, but in the midst of things, enriched by memory,

lighted by anticipation, aware of no trivialities, because acknowledging no finality.

» (1917)

The Tyranny of Facts

Elisabeth Morris

1 Once upon a time, very long, ago, when I was young, I used to dream of all the things I would someday possess. As time went on, the nature of the things I coveted changed, but not the dream of possession. Then, as some of these dreams found their fulfillment, a fundamental reconstruction of ideals took place. I dreamed no longer of possession, but of enfranchisement; I no longer wished for more things, but only for the power to cope with the things I already had—or that had me. And at last my strongest desire was to possess nothing—but friends.

2 Of late, I notice, the same thing that happened in my house has happened in my head. There was a time when I loved to collect in formation. Facts—all facts—were precious to me, and I loved to feel them making piles and stacks and rows in my brain. Every thing was welcome, from the names of the stars to the prepositions that governed the Latin ablative, from the dynasties of Egypt to the geography lists of "state products"—"corn, wheat, and potatoes," "rice, sugar, cotton, and tobacco." While this mania was upon me, dictionaries allured me, cyclopaedias held me spellbound. I was even able to read with interest the annals of the "Swiss Family Robinson," a book which presents more facts per page than any other volume in that great and unclassified mob called "fiction."

3 What were the causes and processes of change I cannot say. Possibly an overdose of facts produced reaction. At all events, the change took place, and the time has now come when, just as I deprecate the arrival of new possessions in my house, even thus do I deplore the stream of information whose constant, relentless flow into my unwilling consciousness I am powerless to prevent. For I find that whereas during my years of enthusiasm for accumulation every-thing combined to help me, now that my endeavors are reversed

the powers arrayed against me are mighty. The Sunday newspaper, which is the embodiment of information invading the last stronghold of peace,—this I can and do bar out of my house; but on week-days the news papers have things their own way. They invade my morning quiet, they disturb my evening calm, they render the male section of my family indifferent to morning coffee and dilatory before evening soup. Nor am I my self exempt from the baleful influence. Various digests of the "world's news" lie constantly upon my table, and I am occasionally weak enough to think it my duty to read them, "so as to be a little intelligent, you know," as a firm-minded aunt of mine is in the habit of saying. In this unwilling endeavor to acquire intelligence I stultify what little of that faculty I may have been origin ally endowed with, I stuff my brain with cotton, in the form of "science brevities," "literary jottings," "religious notes," "political news," and so on. And then for a time a violent reaction sets in, and I eschew all informing books and hie me to Lamb, to Shelley, to Malory, to Homer. These are my joy, my recreation, my tonic.

4 Nor is it only the newspapers and their kind with which I have to contend. My dearest friends are traitors and my foes are they of my own household. For they cling to the possessions of their brains, they are busy amassing more, they survey them with satisfaction and exhibit them with pride, so that I am driven to question, which of us is right? Is the change in me due to growing wisdom or to oncoming senility?

5 In my outdoor life the same issue is constantly presenting itself. I love birds and flowers. In fact, I believe that I honestly love that grand and joyous conglomerate usually called "Nature." There was a time, more over, during that remote period of which I have spoken, when I possessed a respectable amount of information about these matters. Just as, in my lust for physical possessions, I collected butterflies and eggs and flowers, even so in my lust for intellectual possessions I accumulated knowledge—I learned all their names,

I knew all about their wings and their spots and their petals and their seeds and their roots and whatever else appertained to them. It amazes me now when I occasionally stumble upon some record of my former knowledge. I feel like saying, with the old woman in Mother Goose,—

Lawk a massy on me!
This is none of I!

6   But following my feeling of amazement there usually comes one of relief—how glad I am that I don't know all that now! I still love "Nature," but when I have found the lovely flower in the meadow or the deep wood, I do not hasten to pick it and bring it home and analyze it and press it. I am content to lie down beside it a while and enjoy its companionship, its beauty, its fragrance, whatever it has of charm and comeliness, and then I leave it and pass on. When I hear a sweet bird-note, I pause and listen as it comes again and yet again. But I do not pursue the bird with an opera-glass to count its feathers and estimate its dimensions, and then hurry home to my "bird books" to "look it up" and make a marginal note of the date. When I see butterflies fluttering about the lilacs and the syringas and the phlox, I stand quiet and watch them—those huge pale yellow ones banded with black that love to hang about lavender flowers—do they know what a lovely chord of color they strike? those dark ones with blues and greens splashed on their wing-edges, those rich rusty-red ones, with pure silver flashes on their under sides, those little jagged- winged beauties with all the colors of an Oriental rug—old reds, old blues, old yellows—all mottled together. Ah, they are all delightful, and as I watch this favorite and that, holding my breath lest I scare him into flight, I find myself smiling to think, I knew his name once!

7   But most of my friends still know their names. They have opera-glasses and note books, and a prodigious amount of information. They keep tally of the number of birds they see in a day or on a walk or on a drive, of the number of new birds or flowers they

recognize in a season. They call me up by telephone to tell me that the beautiful creature we had seen in a certain tree was, after all, not the Apteryx Americanus, but the Apteryx Warrensis, a much rarer variety of the same species, with longer tail feathers and two more white feathers in the wing than his commonplace cousin.

8   Amid such whirlpools of information I feel that I am unable to hold my own, and so I try to drift out, but now and again I am drawn in, and I find myself growing stupid as I bend over my friends bird books. I give myself headaches looking at their butter-fly cabinets—real butterflies on the phlox and the lilacs never seem to give me headaches.

9   I have said that I do not regret the change in myself, that I would not, if I could, gather up the stores of information I once possessed and refurnish my brain with them,—no, not even if I could arrange them all in order, cleaned and dusted and sorted ready to be used or admired. Let them go! Some of them have already gone alto-gether, thrown away, dropped into cracks, burned up, ground into powder, dissolved into nothing. Some lie, perhaps, piled up in the dusty garrets of my brain, huddled together in formless heaps, or stowed close in the old chests of memory that are never opened. If I searched I might find them, and drag them out, and perhaps among them I might discover some treasures, but I shall never search. I shall let them all lie together in the quiet, dusty twilight, not to be disturbed until the whole mansion, from dim attic to sunlit living-rooms, shall perish to be known no more.

»   (1917)

The Tyranny of Things

Elisabeth Morris

1   Two fifteen-year-old girls stood eyeing one another on first acquaintance. Finally one little girl said, "Which do you like best, people or things?" The other little girl said, "Things." They were friends at once.

2   I suppose we all go through a phase when we like things best; and not only like them, but want to possess them under our hand. The passion for accumulation is upon us. We make "collections," we fill our rooms, our walls, our tables, our desks, with things, things, things.

3   Many people never pass out of this phase. They never see a flower without wanting to pick it and put it in a vase, they never enjoy a book without wanting to own it, nor a picture without wanting to hang it on their walls. They keep photographs of all their friends and kodak albums of all the places they visit, they save all their theater programmes and dinner cards, they bring home all their alpenstocks. Their houses are filled with an undigested mass of things, like the terminal moraine where a glacier dumps at length everything it has picked up during its progress through the lands.

4   But to some of us a day comes when we begin to grow weary of things. We realize that we do not possess them; they possess us. Our books are a burden to us, our pictures have destroyed every restful wall-space, our china is a care, our photographs drive us mad, our programmes and alpenstocks fill us with loathing. We feel stifled with the sense of things, and our problem becomes, not how much we can accumulate, but how much we can do without. We send our books to the village library, and our pictures to the college settlement. Such things as we cannot give away, and have not the courage to destroy, we stack in the garret, where they lie huddled in dim and dusty heaps, removed from our sight, to be

sure, yet still faintly importunate.

5 Then, as we breathe more freely in the clear space that we have made for ourselves, we grow aware that we must not relax our vigilance, or we shall be once more overwhelmed.

6 For it is an age of things. As I walk through the shops at Christmas time and survey their contents, I find it a most depressing spectacle. All of us have too many things already, and here are more! And everybody is going to send some of them to everybody else! I sympathize with one of my friends, who, at the end of the Christmas festivities, said, "If I see another bit of tissue paper and red ribbon, I shall scream."

7 It extends to all our doings. For every event there is a "souvenir." We cannot go to luncheon and meet our friends but we must receive a token to carry away. Even our children cannot have a birthday party, and play games, and eat good things, and be happy. The host must receive gifts from every little guest, and provide in return some little remembrance for each to take home. Truly, on all sides we are beset, and we go lumbering along through life like a ship encrusted with barnacles, which can never cut the waves clean and sure and swift until she has been scraped bare again. And there seems little hope for us this side our last port.

8 And to think that there was a time when folk had not even that hope! When a man's possessions were burned with him, so that he might, forsooth, have them all about him in the next world! Suffocating thought! To think one could not even then be clear of things, and make at least a fresh start! That must, indeed, have been in the childhood of the race.

9 Once upon a time, when I was very tired, I chanced to go away to a little house by the sea. "It is empty," they said, "but you can easily furnish it." Empty! Yes, thank Heaven! Furnish it? Heaven forbid! Its floors were bare, its walls were bare, its tables there were only two in the house were bare. There was nothing in the closets but

books; nothing in the bureau drawers but the smell of clean, fresh wood; nothing in the kitchen but an oil stove, and a few a very few dishes; nothing in the attic but rafters and sunshine, and a view of the sea. After I had been there an hour there descended upon me a great peace, a sense of freedom, of in finite leisure. In the twilight I sat before the flickering embers of the open fire, and looked out through the open door to the sea, and asked myself, "Why?" Then the answer came: I was emancipated from things. There was nothing in the house to demand care, to claim attention, to cumber my consciousness with its insistent, unchanging companionship. There was nothing but a shelter, and outside, the fields and marshes, the shore and the sea. These did not have to be taken down and put up and arranged and dusted and cared for. They were not things at all, they were powers, presences.

10 And so I rested. While the spell was still unbroken, I came away. For broken it would have been, I know, had I not fled first. Even in this refuge the enemy would have pursued me, found me out, encompassed me.

11 If we could but free ourselves once for all, how simple life might become! One of my friends, who, with six young children and only one servant, keeps a spotless house and a soul serene, told me once how she did it. "My dear, once a month I give away every single thing in the house that we do not imperatively need. It sounds wasteful, but I don't believe it really is. Sometimes Jeremiah mourns over missing old clothes, or back numbers of the magazines, but I tell him if he doesn't want to be mated to a gibbering maniac he will let me do as I like."

12 The old monks knew all this very well. One wonders sometimes how they got their power; but go up to Fiesole, and sit a while in one of those little, bare, white-walled cells, and you will begin to understand. If there were any spiritual force in one, it would have to come out there.

13 I have not their courage, and I win no such freedom. I allow myself

to be overwhelmed by the invading host of things, making fitful resistance, but without any real steadiness of purpose. Yet never do I wholly give up the struggle, and in my heart I cherish an ideal, remotely typified by that empty little house beside the sea.

»   (1917)

A Matter of Planes

Elisabeth Morris

1   "My sister and I get along beautifully together: she cares only about the big things of life, and I care only about the little ones." This remark, made to me once by a friend of mine, comes into my mind every now and then, and I am increasingly amused by its astuteness. For nothing seems more capricious than the basis of our harmonious intercourse one with another. We constantly see people whom we would aver to be incompatible, living serenely at peace, while others, whose cordial agreement we would as confidently predict, are quarreling scandalously. I believe my friends remark may throw some light on the matter. It amounts to this: people on the same plane may clash, people on different ones cannot. It is the grade-crossings that make trouble.

2   Let us see how it works. Here are Benedick and I living happily together, although our acquaintances would "never have expected it." We are both of us possessed of strong convictions, but they happen not to concern the same things. For example, I put sugar in my coffee. I think that is the way to take coffee, and of course I always put it in Benedicks cup too. Now Benedick doesn't care,— he would scarcely notice if I dropped an onion in, because he is thinking about civil-service reform and other large matters. As he drinks his coffee he talks to me of these things, which I regard as unquestionably of vital importance, but unquestionably not of vital interest. Yet Benedick talks well, and it is very becoming to him to be deeply in earnest, and so I like to listen to him. Thus we get along together very happily. He accepts my little habits, and I accept his big principles. The adjustment is perfect.

3   On the other hand, there is a certain lady who sometimes visits us. She drinks her coffee without sugar, and she never sits at breakfast with us that she does not evince real uneasiness as she watches the

white cubes being dropped into our steaming cups. Benedick has never even noticed that she is uneasy, but I have, because,—well, because I am living on her plane; for I myself am always conscious of a distinct feeling of annoyance when I see any one put sugar on lettuce. Nor is this the only ground of discord between us. She has the habit of rising at half-past six every morning, and taking a cold bath before breakfast. She is never late. I often am, and I loathe cold baths, except in the ocean. Accordingly, when I come down, I find her awaiting me, covered with meritoriousness as with a garment, and I feel myself her inferior, a feeling which I resent but can not escape. I find no refuge in philosophy, for I have no more philosophy than she has. No, we are on the same plane, and we are always colliding.

4   On the other hand, Benedick likes her very well, but for his part cannot get through a meal comfortably with his uncle, because they disagree about trusts and the tariff. Yet his uncle and I always enjoy each other's society. He takes three lumps of sugar in his coffee and none at all on his lettuce; he regularly oversleeps the breakfast hour and apologizes handsomely for it afterwards. He has, in fact, what I consider a comfortable set of habits, and his theories do not disturb me. Personally, I find it pleasant to live with people who will let me arrange the unimportant features of life, while I am quite ready to let them settle what one of my teachers used to call its "cosmic principles." I can understand one's enduring martyrdom for the sake of details of taste, but not for such large matters as Truth or the Hereafter, which seem to me abundantly able to take care of themselves.

5   I wonder if this explains why men are less apt to quarrel with women than with other men, and women less apt to quarrel with men than with other women. For the lives of men and women are doubtless on quite different planes; they are not apt to feel strongly about the same things, and thus each is indulgent toward the other's convictions, not being deeply touched by them. Have

you ever noticed at a dinner-party, when one of the men is telling a good story, the difference between the attitudes of the other men and of the women? The women—except perhaps the wife of the speaker—listen easily, receptively; the men listen restlessly, each alert for a chance to follow up the tale with one of his own. For it is perfectly well understood that women are not required to tell good stories at dinner, and so a woman can enjoy them all irresponsibly, while a man feels in each one something very like a challenge.

6   On the other hand, when either sex invades the other sphere, there is apt to be trouble. We all know how a woman, the ordinary, normal woman, feels when the man attempts to "interfere" in the household; and a man, the ordinary, normal man, has a similar objection to womens invading his province. In Germany, at a university function some years ago, an old professor in conversation with a young American woman expressed himself rather positively on some economic question. She, being fairly well grounded in economics, ventured to differ, and began to give her reasons for so doing, when he interrupted her with a gesture of surprise and irritation, and the remark, "I am not accustomed to hear myself contradicted by young women."

7   But I suppose some one may object, "Why must people on the same plane inevitably collide? Why cannot they run companionably parallel?" And indeed this has an attractive sound; but people's lives do not run on artificial tracks. They may move along easily side by side for a while, but then crash! The collision comes.

8   If you still doubt, try two experiments. Find two people deeply interested in theological theory, and apparently in agreement, and set them discussing the matter with each other in a really exhaustive way. See if they do not separate with some little mutual disapproval, if not distrust. "Ah!—Mr.——is not so sound as I had supposed." Then, to make the test on the little things of life, take two people the most harmonious possible, find them in an amiable mood, I will even allow you to give them a good dinner first, and

then set them the task of choosing wallpapers for their country home. Need I describe the outcome?

9 Ah, no! Our only safety lies in non-conflicting levels. You who are entering on a matrimonial or otherwise friendly compact, put not your trust in a harmony based on positive agreement: it is shifting sand beneath your feet. Ground your happiness in a nice dovetailing of eager conviction with tolerant indifference, and you are safe for a lifetime.

» (1917)

On Laziness

Christopher Morley

1   To-day we rather intended to write an essay on Laziness, but were too indolent to do so.

2   The sort of thing we had in mind to write would have been exceedingly persuasive. We intended to discourse a little in favour of a greater appreciation of Indolence as a benign factor in human affairs.

3   It is our observation that every time we get into trouble it is due to not having been lazy enough. Unhappily, we were born with a certain fund of energy. We have been hustling about for a number of years now, and it doesn't seem to get us anything but tribulation. Henceforward we are going to make a determined effort to be more languid and demure. It is the bustling man who always gets put on committees, who is asked to solve the problems of other people and neglect his own.

4   The man who is really, thoroughly, and philosophically slothful is the only thoroughly happy man. It is the happy man who benefits the world. The conclusion is inescapable.

5   We remember a saying about the meek inheriting the earth. The truly meek man is the lazy man. He is too modest to believe that any ferment and hubbub of his can ameliorate the earth or assuage the perplexities of humanity.

6   O. Henry said once that one should be careful to distinguish laziness from dignified repose. Alas, that was a mere quibble. Laziness is always dignified, it is always reposeful. Philosophical laziness, we mean. The kind of laziness that is based upon a carefully reasoned analysis of experience. Acquired laziness. We have no respect for those who were born lazy; it is like being born a millionaire: they cannot appreciate their bliss. It is the man who has hammered his

laziness out of the stubborn material of life for whom we chant praise and allelulia.

7 The laziest man we know—we do not like to mention his name, as the brutal world does not yet recognize sloth at its community value—is one of the greatest poets in this country; one of the keenest satirists; one of the most rectilinear thinkers. He began life in the customary hustling way. He was always too busy to enjoy himself. He became surrounded by eager people who came to him to solve their problems. "It's a queer thing," he said sadly; "no one ever comes to me asking for help in solving my problems." Finally the light broke upon him. He stopped answering letters, buying lunches for casual friends and visitors from out of town, he stopped lending money to old college pals and frittering his time away on all the useless minor matters that pester the good-natured. He sat down in a secluded café with his cheek against a seidel of dark beer and began to caress the universe with his intellect.

8 The most damning argument against the Germans is that they were not lazy enough. In the middle of Europe, a thoroughly disillusioned, indolent and delightful old continent, the Germans were a dangerous mass of energy and bumptious push. If the Germans had been as lazy, as indifferent, and as righteously laissez-fairish as their neighbours, the world would have been spared a great deal.

9 People respect laziness. If you once get a reputation for complete, immovable, and reckless indolence the world will leave you to your own thoughts, which are generally rather interesting.

10 Doctor Johnson, who was one of the world's great philosophers, was lazy. Only yesterday our friend the Caliph showed us an extraordinarily interesting thing. It was a little leather-bound notebook in which Boswell jotted down memoranda of his talks with the old doctor. These notes he afterward worked up into the immortal Biography. And lo and behold, what was the very first entry in this treasured little relic?

11 Doctor Johnson told me in going to Ilam from Ashbourne, 22 September, 1777, that the way the plan of his Dictionary came to be addressed to Lord Chesterfield was this: He had neglected to write it by the time appointed. Dodsley suggested a desire to have it addressed to Lord C. Mr. J. laid hold of this as an excuse for delay, that it might be better done perhaps, and let Dodsley have his desire. Mr. Johnson said to his friend, Doctor Bathurst: "Now if any good comes of my addressing to Lord Chesterfield it will be ascribed to deep policy and address, when, in fact, it was only a casual excuse for laziness."

12 Thus we see that it was sheer laziness that led to the greatest triumph of Doctor Johnson's life, the noble and memorable letter to Chesterfield in 1775.

13 Mind your business is a good counsel; but mind your idleness also. It's a tragic thing to make a business of your mind. Save your mind to amuse yourself with.

14 The lazy man does not stand in the way of progress. When he sees progress roaring down upon him he steps nimbly out of the way. The lazy man doesn't (in the vulgar phrase) pass the buck. He lets the buck pass him. We have always secretly envied our lazy friends. Now we are going to join them. We have burned our boats or our bridges or whatever it is that one burns on the eve of a momentous decision.

15 Writing on this congenial topic has roused us up to quite a pitch of enthusiasm and energy.

» (1920)

On Visiting Bookshops

Christopher Morley

1 It is a curious thing that so many people only go into a book-shop when they happen to need some particular book. Do they never drop in for a little innocent carouse and refreshment? There are some knightly souls who even go so far as to make their visits to bookshops a kind of chivalrous errantry at large. They go in not because they need any certain volume, but because they feel that there may be some book that needs them. Some wistful, little forgotten sheaf of loveliness, long pining away on an upper shelf— why not ride up, fling her across your charger (or your charge account), and gallop away. Be a little knightly, you book-lovers!

2 The lack of intelligence with which people use bookshops is, one supposes, no more flagrant than the lack of intelligence with which we use all the rest of the machinery of civilization. In this age, and particularly in this city, we haven't time to be intelligent.

3 A queer thing about books, if you open your heart to them, is the instant and irresistible way they follow you with their appeal. You know at once, if you are clairvoyant in these matters (libre-voyant, one might say), when you have met your book. You may dally and evade, you may go on about your affairs, but the paragraph of prose your eye fell upon, or the snatch of verses, or perhaps only the spirit and flavour of the volume, more divined than reasonably noted, will follow you. A few lines glimpsed on a page may alter your whole trend of thought for the day, reverse the currents of the mind, change the profile of the city. The other evening, on a subway car, we were reading Walter de la Mare's interesting little essay about Rupert Brooke. His discussion of children, their dreaming ways, their exalted simplicity and absorption, changed the whole tenor of our voyage by some magical chemistry of thought. It was no longer a wild, barbaric struggle with our fellowmen, but a venture of faith

and recompense, taking us home to the bedtime of a child.

4 The moment when one meets a book and knows, beyond shadow of doubt, that that book must be his—not necessarily now, but some time—is among the happiest excitements of the spirit. An indescribable virtue effuses from some books. One can feel the radiations of an honest book long before one sees it, if one has a sensitive pulse for such affairs. Its honour and truth will speak through the advertising. Its mind and heart will cry out even underneath the extravagance of jacket-blurbings. Some shrewd soul, who understands books, remarked some time ago on the editorial page of the Sun's book review that no superlative on a jacket had ever done the book an atom of good. He was right, as far as the true bookster is concerned. We choose our dinner not by the wrappers, but by the veining and gristle of the meat within. The other day, prowling about a bookshop, we came upon two paper-bound copies of a little book of poems by Alice Meynell. They had been there for at least two years. We had seen them before, a year or more ago, but had not looked into them fearing to be tempted. This time we ventured. We came upon two poems—"To O, Of Her Dark Eyes," and "A Wind of Clear Weather in England." The book was ours— or rather, we were its, though we did not yield at once. We came back the next day and got it. We are still wondering how a book like that could stay in the shop so long. Once we had it, the day was different. The sky was sluiced with a clearer blue, air and sunlight blended for a keener intake of the lungs, faces seen along the street moved us with a livelier shock of interest and surprise. The wind that moved over Sussex and blew Mrs. Meynell's heart into her lines was still flowing across the ribs and ledges of our distant scene.

5 There is no mistaking a real book when one meets it. It is like falling in love, and like that colossal adventure it is an experience of great social import. Even as the tranced swain, the book-lover yearns to tell others of his bliss. He writes letters about it, adds it to the postscript of all manner of communications, intrudes it into

telephone messages, and insists on his friends writing down the title of the find. Like the simple-hearted betrothed, once certain of his conquest, "I want you to love her, too!" It is a jealous passion also. He feels a little indignant if he finds that any one else has discovered the book, too. He sees an enthusiastic review—very likely in The New Republic—and says, with great scorn, "I read the book three months ago." There are even some perversions of passion by which a book-lover loses much of his affection for his pet if he sees it too highly commended by some rival critic.

6   This sharp ecstasy of discovering books for one's self is not always widespread. There are many who, for one reason or another, prefer to have their books found out for them. But for the complete zealot nothing transcends the zest of pioneering for himself. And therefore working for a publisher is, to a certain type of mind, a never-failing fascination. As H. M. Tomlinson says in "Old Junk," that fascinating collection of sensitive and beautifully poised sketches which came to us recently with a shock of thrilling delight:

> To come upon a craft rigged so, though at her moorings and with
> sails furled, her slender poles upspringing from the bright plane
> of a brimming harbour, is to me as rare and sensational a delight
> as the rediscovery, when idling with a book, of a favourite
> lyric.

7   To read just that passage, and the phrase the bright plane of a brimming harbour, is one of those "rare and sensational delights" that set the mind moving on lovely journeys of its own, and mark off visits to a bookshop not as casual errands of reason, but as necessary acts of devotion. We visit bookshops not so often to buy any one special book, but rather to rediscover, in the happier and more expressive words of others, our own encumbered soul.

»   (1920)

Safety Pins

Christopher Morley Edited by John Pfannkuchen

1   Ligature of infancy, healing engine of emergency, base and mainstay of our civilization—we celebrate the safety pin.

2   What would we do without safety pins? Is it not odd to think, looking about us on our fellowmen (bearded realtors, would-be poets, plump and ruddy policemen, even the cheerful dusky creature who runs the elevator and whistles "Oh, What a Pal Was Mary" as the clock draws near 6 P. M.)—all these were first housed and swaddled and made seemly with a paper of safety pins. How is it that the inventor who first conferred this great gift on the world is not known by name for the admiration and applause of posterity? Was it not the safety pin that made the world safe for infancy?

3   There will be some, mayhap, to set up the button as rival to the safety pin in service to humanity. But our homage bends toward the former. Not only was it our shield and buckler when we were too puny and impish to help ourselves, but it is also (now we are parent) symbol of many a hard-fought field, where we have campaigned all over the white counterpane of a large bed to establish an urchin in his proper gear, while he kicked and scrambled, witless of our dismay. It is fortunate, pardee, that human memory does not extend backward to the safety pin era—happily the recording carbon sheet of the mind is not inserted on the roller of experience until after the singular humiliations of earliest childhood have passed. Otherwise our first recollection would doubtless be of the grimly flushed large face of a resolute parent, bending hotly downward in effort to make both ends meet while we wambled and waggled in innocent, maddening sport. In those days when life was (as George Herbert puts it) "assorted sorrows, anguish of all sizes," the safety pin was the only thing that raised us above the bandar-log. No wonder the antique schoolmen used to enjoy computing the number of angels

that might dance on the point of a pin. But only archangels would be worthy to pirouette on a safety pin, which is indeed mightier than the sword. When Adam delved and Eve did spin, what did they do for a safety pin?

4 Great is the stride when an infant passes from the safety pin period to the age of buttons. There are three ages of human beings in this matter: (1) Safety pins, (2) Buttons, (3) Studs, or (for females) Hooks and Eyes. Now there is an interim in the life of man when he passes away from safety pins, and, for a season, knows them not—save as mere convenience in case of breakdown. He thinks of them, in his antic bachelor years, as merely the wrecking train of the sartorial system, a casual conjunction for pyjamas, or an impromptu hoist for small clothes. Ah! with humility and gratitude he greets them again later, seeing them at their true worth, the symbol of integration for the whole social fabric. Women, with their intuitive wisdom, are more subtle in this subject. They never wholly outgrow safety pins, and though they love to ornament them with jewellery, precious metal, and enamels, they are naught but safety pins after all. Some ingenious philosopher could write a full tractate on woman in her relation to pins—hairpins, clothes pins, rolling pins, hatpins.

5 Only a bachelor, as we have implied, scoffs at pins. Hamlet remarked, after seeing the ghost, and not having any Sir Oliver Lodge handy to reassure him, that he did not value his life at a pin's fee. Pope, we believe, coined the contemptuous phrase, "I care not a pin." The pin has never been done justice in the world of poetry. As one might say, the pin has had no Pindar. Of course there is the old saw about see a pin and pick it up, all the day you'll have good luck. This couplet, barbarous as it is in its false rhyme, points (as Mother Goose generally does) to a profound truth. When you see a pin, you must pick it up. In other words, it is on the floor, where pins generally are. Their instinctive affinity for terra firma makes one wonder why they, rather than the apple, did not suggest the

law of gravitation to someone long before Newton.

6   Incidentally, of course, the reason why Adam and Eve were forbidden to pick the apple was that it was supposed to stay on the tree until it fell, and Adam would then have had the credit of spotting the principle of gravitation.

7   Much more might be said about pins, touching upon their curious capacity for disappearing, superstitions concerning them, usefulness of hatpins or hairpins as pipe-cleaners, usefulness of pins to schoolboys, both when bent for fishing and when filed to an extra point for use on the boy in the seat in front (honouring him in the breech, as Hamlet would have said) and their curious habits of turning up in unexpected places, undoubtedly caught by pins in their long association with the lovelier sex. But of these useful hyphens of raiment we will merely conclude by saying that those interested in the pin industry will probably emigrate to England, for we learn from the Encyclopædia Britannica that in that happy island pins are cleaned by being boiled in weak beer. Let it not be forgotten, however, that of all kinds, the safety is the King Pin.

»   (1920)

A Proposal to Girdle the Earth

Nellie Bly

1   What gave me the idea? It is sometimes difficult to tell exactly what gives birth to an idea. Ideas are the chief stock in trade of newspaper writers and generally they are the scarcest stock in market, but they do come occasionally, This idea came to me one Sunday. I had spent a greater part of the day and half the night vainly trying to fasten on some idea for a newspaper article. It was my custom to think up ideas on Sunday and lay them before my editor for his approval or disapproval on Monday. But ideas did not come that day and three o'clock in the morning found me weary and with an aching head tossing about in my bed. At last tired and provoked at my slowness in finding a subject, something for the week's work, I thought fretfully: "I wish I was at the other end of the earth!"

2   "And why not?" the thought came: "I need a vacation; why not take a trip around the world?" It is easy to see how one thought followed another. The idea of a trip around the world pleased me and I added: "If I could do it as quickly as Phileas Fogg did, I should go." Then I wondered if it were possible to do the trip eighty days and afterwards I went easily off to sleep with the determination to know before I saw my bed again if Phileas Fogg's record could be broken. I went to a steamship company's office that day and made a selection of time tables. Anxiously I sat down and went over them and if I had found the elixir of life I should not have felt better than I did when I conceived a hope that a tour of the world might be made in even less than eighty days. I approached my editor rather timidly on the subject. I was afraid that he would think the idea too wild and visionary.

3   "Have you any ideas?" he asked, as I sat down by his desk.

4   "One," I answered quietly. He sat toying with his pens, waiting for me to continue, so I blurted out: "I want to go around the world!"

5   "Well?" he said, inquiringly looking up with a faint smile in his kind eyes.

6   "I want to go around in eighty days or less. I think I can beat Phileas Fogg's record. May I try it?"

7   To my dismay he told me that in the office they had thought of this same idea before and the intention was to send a man. However he offered me the consolation that he would favor my going, and then we went to talk with the business manager about it. "It is impossible for you to do it," was the terrible verdict. "In the first place you are a woman and would need a protector, and even if it were possible for you to travel alone you would need to carry so much baggage that it would detain you in making rapid changes. Besides you speak nothing but English, so there is no use talking about it; no one but a man can do this."

8   "Very well," I said angrily, "Start the man, and I'll start the same day for some other newspaper and beat him."

9   "I believe you would," he said slowly. I would not say that this had any influence on their decision, but I do know that before we parted I was made happy by the promise that if any one was commissioned to make the trip, I should be that one.

10 After I had made my arrangements to go, other important projects for gathering news came up, and this rather visionary idea was put aside for a while. One cold, wet evening, a year after this discussion, I received a little note asking me to come to the office at once. A summons, late in the afternoon, was such an unusual thing to me that I was to be excused if I spent all my time on the way to the office wondering what I was to be scolded for. I went in and sat down beside the editor waiting for him to speak. He looked up from the paper on which he was writing and asked quietly: "Can you start around the world day after tomorrow?"

11 "I can start this minute," I answered, quickly trying to stop the rapid beating of my heart.

12 "We did think of starting you on the City of Paris tomorrow morning, so as to give you ample time to catch the mail train out of London. There is a chance if the Augusta Victoria, which sails the morning afterwards, has rough weather of your failing to connect with the mail train."

13 "I will take my chances on the Augusta Victoria, and save one extra day," I said. The next morning I went to Ghormley, the fashionable dressmaker, to order a dress. It was after eleven o'clock when I got there and it took but very few moments to tell him what I wanted. I always have a comfortable feeling that nothing is impossible if one applies a certain amount of energy in the right direction. When I want things done, which is always at the last moment, and I am met with such an answer: "It's too late. I hardly think it can be done;" I simply say: "Nonsense! If you want to do it, you can do it. The question is, do you want to do it?"

14 I have never met the man or woman yet who was not aroused by that answer into doing their very best. If we want good work from others or wish to accomplish anything ourselves, it will never do to harbor a doubt as to the result of an enterprise. So, when I went to Ghormley's, I said to him: "I want a dress by this evening."

15 "Very well," he answered as unconcernedly as if it were an everyday thing for a young woman to order a gown on a few hours' notice.

16 "I want a dress that will stand constant wear for three months," I added, and then let the responsibility rest on him. Bringing out several different materials he threw them in artistic folds over a small table, studying the effect in a pier glass before which he stood. He did not become nervous or hurried. All the time that he was trying the different effects of the materials, he kept up a lively and half humorous conversation. In a few moments he had selected a plain blue broadcloth and a quiet plaid camel's-hair as the most durable and suitable combination for a traveling gown.

17 Before I left, probably one o'clock, I had my first fitting. When I

returned at five o'clock for a second fitting, the dress was finished. I considered this promptness and speed a good omen and quite in keeping with the project. After leaving Ghormley's I went to a shop and ordered an ulster. Then going to another dressmaker's, I ordered a lighter dress to carry with me to be worn in the land where I would find summer. I bought one hand-bag with the determination to confine my baggage to its limit.

18 That night there was nothing to do but write to my few friends a line of farewell and to pack the hand-bag. Packing that bag was the most difficult undertaking of my life; there was so much to go into such little space. I got everything in at last except the extra dress. Then the question resolved itself into this: I must either add a parcel to my baggage or go around the world in and with one dress. I always hated parcels so I sacrificed the dress, but I brought out a last summer's silk bodice and after considerable squeezing managed to crush it into the hand-bag.

19 I think that I went away one of the most superstitious of girls. My editor had told me the day before the trip had been decided upon of an inauspicious dream he had had. It seemed that I came to him and told him I was going to run a race. Doubting my ability as a runner, he thought he turned his back so that he should not witness the race. He heard the band play, as it does on such occasions, and heard the applause that greeted the finish. Then I came to him with my eyes filled with tears and said: "I have lost the race."

20 "I can translate that dream," I said, when he finished; "I will start to secure some news and some one else will beat me." When I was told the next day that I was to go around the world I felt a prophetic awe steal over me. I feared that Time would win the race and that I should not make the tour in eighty days or less. Nor was my health good when I was told to go around the world in the shortest time possible at that season of the year. For almost a year I had been a daily sufferer from headache, and only the week previous I had consulted a number of eminent physicians fearing

that my health was becoming impaired by too constant application to work. I had been doing newspaper work for almost three years, during which time I had not enjoyed one day's vacation. It is not surprising then that I looked on this trip as a most delightful and much needed rest.

21 The evening before I started I went to the office and was given £200 in English gold and Bank of England notes. The gold I carried in my pocket. The Bank of England notes were placed in a chamois-skin bag which I tied around my neck. Besides this I took some American gold and paper money to use at different ports as a test to see if American money was known outside of America. Down in the bottom of my hand-bag was a special passport, number 247, signed by James G. Blaine, Secretary of State.

22 Someone suggested that a revolver would be a good companion piece for the passport, but I had such a strong belief in the world's greeting me as I greeted it, that I refused to arm myself. I knew if my conduct was proper I should always find men ready to protect me, let them be Americans, English, French, German or anything else.

23 It is quite possible to buy tickets in New York for the entire trip, but I thought that I might be compelled to change my route at almost any point, so the only transportation I had provided on leaving New York was my ticket to London. When I went to the office to say good-bye, I found that no itinerary had been made of my contemplated trip and there was some doubt as to whether the mail train which I expected to take to Brindisi, left London every Friday night. Nor did we know whether the week of my expected arrival in London was the one in which it connected with the ship for India or the ship for China. In fact when I arrived at Brindisi and found the ship was bound for Australia, I was the most surprised girl in the world. I followed a man who had been sent to a steamship company's office to try to make out a schedule and help them arrange one as best they could on this side of the water. How near

it came to being correct can be seen later on.

24 I have been asked very often since my return how many changes of clothing I took in my solitary hand-bag. Some have thought I took but one; others think I carried silk which occupies but little space, and others have asked if I did not buy what I needed at the different ports. One never knows the capacity of an ordinary hand-satchel until dire necessity compels the exercise of all one's ingenuity to reduce every thing to the smallest possible compass. In mine I was able to pack two traveling caps, three veils, a pair of slippers, a complete outfit of toilet articles, ink-stand, pens, pencils, and copy-paper, pins, needles and thread, a dressing gown, a tennis blazer, a small flask and a drinking cup, several complete changes of underwear, a liberal supply of handkerchiefs and fresh ruchings and most bulky and uncompromising of all, a jar of cold cream to keep my face from chapping in the varied climates I should encounter. That jar of cold cream was the bane of my existence. It seemed to take up more room than everything else in the bag and was always getting into just the place that would keep me from closing the satchel. Over my arm I carried a silk waterproof, the only provision I made against rainy weather.

25 After-experience showed me that I had taken too much rather than too little baggage. At every port where I stopped at I could have bought anything from a ready-made dress down, except possibly at Aden, and as I did not visit the shops there I cannot speak from knowledge. The possibilities of having any laundry work done during my rapid progress was one which had troubled me a good deal before starting. I had equipped myself on the theory that only once or twice in my journey would I be able to secure the services of a laundress. I knew that on the railways it would be impossible, but the longest railroad travel was the two days spent between London and Brindisi, and the four days between San Francisco and New York. On the Atlantic steamers they do no washing. On the Peninsular and Oriental steamers—which everyone calls the P.&O.

boats—between Brindisi and China, the quartermaster turns out each day a wash that would astonish the largest laundry in America. Even if no laundry work was done on the ships, there are at all of the ports where they stop plenty of experts waiting to show what Orientals can do in the washing line. Six hours is ample time for them to perform their labors and when they make a promise to have work done in a certain time, they are prompt to the minute. Probably it is because they have no use for clothes themselves, but appreciate at its full value the money they are to receive for their labor. Their charges, compared with laundry prices in New York, are wonderfully low.

26 So much for my preparations. It will be seen that if one is traveling simply for the sake of traveling and not for the purpose of impressing one's fellow passengers, the problem of baggage becomes a very simple one. On one occasion—in Hong Kong, where I was asked to an official dinner—I regretted not having an evening dress with me, but the loss of that dinner was a very small matter when compared with the responsibilities and worries I escaped by not having a lot of trunks and boxes to look after.

» (1908)

Arachne, or the Housekeeper

Grace Little Rhys

1   With the ceaseless growth of populations, life grows less and less
kindly for the woman and the child. The happy village life, with its
freedoms, its play-places for the children, its crafts and its songs,
has gradually decayed away. From causes deep-rooted in the appetites of mankind and common to all races, the people are driven
more and more into cities. There the stony ways under foot, the
closed houses like barren cliffs on either hand, the factory walls
and chimneys forever multiplying, the strange machinery of iron
and steel—look grimly on the woman and the child. The monster
greed, who lies at the bottom of every human heart, steps out
boldly under the sun, clothed in armour of stone and steel, defying
nature, kindness, beauty, art, handicraft, and all the fair simplicities
that constitute the natural life.

2   Since our conditioning is everywhere rapidly changing, since,
among the noisy, pushing multitudes, the weakest not only go to
the wall (as our proverb has it), but even down to the pit the case
of woman needs to be newly stated. She must know in what today
consists her virtue and her strength; what are her faculties, which
way lies her path, what she shall desire, what she shall taste and
what refuse.

3   Very many are the offices and faculties of women; we can hardly
count her different guises, so many does she wear in this tumult
of increasing life. We recognize her as woman, the keeper of the
house ; woman, the people's servant; woman, the labourer; woman,
the industrial slave; woman, the artist and follower of the crafts;
woman, the healer; woman, the worshipper of Athene, mistress
of all knowledges; woman, the priestess; woman, the counsellor,
mother of mankind; woman, daughter of folly; woman, daughter of hell. Perhaps in all her manifold impersonations, woman is

most completely herself in her immemorial office as keeper of the house. Realizing, as we can, the immemorial an elemental type of the housekeeper, we may consider afresh what are her functions, what her material of life, to what degree of honour she is born.

4   Apart from the particular faculty of any artist, the degree of honour he receives is proportionate to the beauty and permanence of his material. The older artists relied for their ultimate greatness of reputation on the purity and lasting qualities of the colours they used. If their work had soon faded away, so would their honour.

5   The housekeeper works in the most perishable material of all: it dies under her hand at night and must be renewed each morning. For builders in the frail and insubstantial, the housekeeper and Arachne, the spider, might make a match of it. The spider is incessantly spinning a web from her own inner store, constantly renewing it, constantly seeing her labour swept away. The housekeeper's work, scarcely ended when she lies down at night, begins afresh with every dawn. She works in such material as water and fire, flour and soap, needles and thread, roses, and the broom. She is the link between man and the eternal simplicities.

6   Of her completed works, some of the most important are eatable and meant to be demolished, for she is bond-woman to the appetites of her house-mates. She fights one long pitched battle with decay and many-legged depredators. But her enemy of enemies is dust: dust that forever rises in the footsteps of man. Out of doors sweet Mother Nature, who abhors dust, lays her live green carpet wherever she possibly can, and securely binds it down. When her green carpet fails, then the true terrors of dust are seen; we get the charging dust-storm a mile high, rattling like giant artillery and slaying all before it. Within doors, but for the cleansing hand of the housekeeper, life would be hideous. The labours of Sisyphus are hers—the enemy dust, slain yesterday, rises again to-day, and will rise again tomorrow.

7   With such materials and such labour what pictures does our house-

keeper create—pictures to hang forever in the memory of those who behold them. We have all seen them; they are common to every nation. The sun at the open window, crossing the floor, and the straight-made bed. The child's face at the morning meal. The flower slowly opening in the vase. The lamp shining at night. The voice of welcome in the ready-opened door. The thrill of music in the house. The food fairly laid upon the board. Elements of life, every one of them, perfect and eternal, beautiful as art.

8 Although this task of hers is that of a priestess and comparable to the work done by Mother Nature herself, it is not always seen so by men, nor even by herself. When called into the great market of the world to show her finished work, because of which she should have honour, behold, her hands are empty: there is nothing to show: she is of little account: her face is tired and her hair is grey. She has grown wise through the touch and feel of things, but she does not express her wisdom, as those do who have grown wise mainly from books. She stands silent, her voice unheard in the world's uproar.

9 Yet if you but stop a moment to consider that wholesome figure, she will presently appear to you to be significant: there is something there of the priestess, something of mystery and dignity: is she not an artist in life? Her art is the weaving of the indestructible out of the destructible. Out of such material as garments and draperies, comely meals, renewals of the bright hearth where love sits and warms herself, good counsel and the touch of the restoring hand, she moulds and stays up human life. She is the life-giver and the life-preserver.

10 You see, in that comely figure of the good housekeeper who steals neglected into the world's market-place, who is unpaid, and taken for granted, there hides an artist of rare achievement. Like Arachne, the spider, she has woven out of her very vitals a web of life. Here and there may be knots and flaws and tangles, yet in spite of them it will be found an acceptable piece of work; golden threads run through it; and when it is laid down as a carpet for the feet of the

Lord of Life, it shines well enough and is on the whole worthy to take his footprints.

»   (1920)

Daughters of the Air

Grace Little Rhys

1   Skies are not yet gone out of fashion in the country. Down there an intelligent person can tell by looking at them whether or no it is likely to rain. There are also outlandish people who will tell you the time by merely casting a glance at the sun on its way. But in the streets of our cities, where rain can be avoided by merely getting into an omnibus, and where clocks are nearly as plentiful as trees in the country, very few people are ever to be seen looking at the sky.

2   For one thing our necks are not built on at quite the right angle; though better off in that way than the cow, we are scarcely so nicely adapted as the thrush. Our eyes too are hardly strong enough; they should wear eagle's hoods for sky-gazing. Then there is the human drama of the stream of passing faces to distract the mind: for female eyes there is the bait of the shop-window; for men there is the craft of getting and having.

3   And yet that heavenly parallelogram across which pieces of shorn cloud continually pass, is well worth an upward glance. What a pity that natural wonders so soon cease to astonish. For a few seasons the child is astonished at the wind. For ten or twelve winters the snow is a wonder. For a while only the voyaging of the clouds is matter for questions. I know a little child who used to be afraid to go out on a dull day for fear the heavy clouds should fall on her and crush her. Now she knows them securely balanced on the wind's back, and her fear is changed to delight in their extravagances. As the years go on she will cease to marvel, and look upward not so often.

4   Eyes and mind soon become accustomed to a miracle that happens every day and in time notice no more. I do believe that if our city skies could suddenly become early Italian, deep blue, studded with flights of red-robed angels blowing on golden trumpets, and dotted

with winged, bodiless cherubs, we should soon grow used to it, and saying, "It is only the angels," our men would hurry head down to their offices and our women to their beloved shops.

5 And yet the changing moods of our skies should be wonderful enough to hold us spell-bound for a moment, quite irrespective of any augury of the weather. Our brothers the clouds are great and beautiful creatures, wonderful in themselves, most wonderful in their attributes.

6 For instance, who could suppose that a mist of vapour could hold fire in its heart? Who could have imagined, if they had not seen, the sheets of flame that they can pour out; who that had not heard it could have invented the truly appalling noise of the thunder? It ought to be as astounding as if an exploding pistol should be born of a down pillow, or a dagger of a lady's ball-dress. Any human creature caught in a thunderstorm without previous knowledge of the subject would probably go mad or die of terror.

7 The miracle of the noise of the thunder is only fully appreciated by those who know in what deep silence clouds pursue their journeys. Climb alone on mountains, walk in and out of clouds: stand still and let a huge cloud travel soundlessly down upon you, on a calm day when no wind stirs, and you will know the ghostliness of motion without sound. Not only do the clouds bear down upon you in solemn stillness, but they muffle up and choke the waves of any sound that may be produced within their borders.

8 I remember one day walking through a cloud that stood upon the broad side of Moel Gamelyn; it was a thick, pale grey cloud, inexpressibly solemn and still. But a foot of the mountain road could be seen at a time; one plunged forward among the folds of grey curtains that closed again behind. All at once, without any warning, there started out of the mist a man in a peasant's dress, who led by a cavesson a powerful bay horse. Appearing thus suddenly in that remote deserted region, in such stillness, and wrapped all about in that investiture of grey, man and horse looked the appari-

tion of a dream. The horse snorted and plunged on seeing me and the man saluted me with a hoarse, "Boreu da y chi." ["Good day to you."]

9   The next moment they were out of sight, covered in folds of mist, even the sound of the big horse's hoofs swallowed up and lost.

10 On issuing out of the cloud, I found that every minutest hair of the rough tweed dress I wore was embroidered in beads of vapour, so small as to be hardly visible. Each one, shining beside its neighbour, was woven for the moment into a silver cloth; the tissue of this cloth might be fragile and evanescent, but it was somehow related to the stars.

11 And then the wonder of the rain. A colder river of air touches these fire-chariots that run on silent wheels across our skies, and, behold! a million dropping tears, rainbow carriers, travelers of the sky; or if the cloud is heavy, and large drops are driven slantwise on a rapid wind, we have a million million crystal daggers that strike with a sweet sound on the window-pane; how they can sting, these daggers, the uncovered cheek and neck of the field-labourer know only too well.

12 The rain is not all. Let but a cold wind lay its miracle-working finger on these soft beaded masses and see what happens: the hidden power awakes, the crystals set; clear gleaming stars, snow wheels, banded feathers, ice flowers, ferns and plumes, in hosts upon hosts fall down in silence; so that to-morrow mere men might walk on a sweet-smelling, snow-white floor, that was the embroidered drapery of the heavens of yesterday.

13 In spite of all their tricks of dissolution clouds are corporate creatures; else why have they that core of fire underneath those robes of snow? They are brotherly with one another; one cloud by itself in the heavens is lonely and is sure to set sail to the first wind and hurry off to seek out its fellows. Clouds love to roll together in masses; those are heavy days when they stand tumbling, a mile

deep, overhead. On such days one thinks of the fate of the planet Venus, rolled round and round for ever in an undivided veil of silver grey: how pale the flowers must grow in that cloudy land! On such days it is a comfort to think of the upper side of our earthly cloud roof, where floods of golden sunshine roll upon a white floor. What a place for sport, if we could only get there!

14 Long ago clouds were credited with a strange knowledge and foreknowledge of human affairs. At the time of the plague the people of London used to troop into the fields to watch the skies, which showed affrighting shapes and colours and lights.

15 "I did see Mr. Christopher Love beheaded on Tower Hill, in a delicate, clear day," writes Aubrey; "about half an hour after his head was struck off the clouds gathered blacker and blacker; and such terrible claps of thunder came that I never heard greater."

16 I have seen as great and more certain a wonder than this when sitting to watch the tide fill in among the Essex marshes. There in still blue weather the salt blue streams rise noiselessly in the brown channels. On such a day, while watching the quiet spreading of those inland seas, I have heard the sound of a gun from Shoeburyness suddenly break up the silent peace with its sinister reminder of man's cruelties. I have seen the very daylight obscured by that voice of murder.

17 Far enough away the clouds must have been resting on distant seas in that still blue weather, and yet they came quickly. To see these formless grey creatures rushing up out of the clear circle of the horizon and to hear presently their deep, woolly-throated bass echoing the sound of the artillery in outrageous symphony, brings to the mind strange food for thought. So may men's enmities distract the heavens, and the clouds themselves fall to war when men are at variance.

» (1920)

On Scipio's Villa

Lucius Annaeus Seneca

1   I am resting at the country-house which once belonged to Scipio Africanus himself; and I write to you after doing reverence to his spirit and to an altar which I am incline to think is the tomb of that great warrior. That his soul has indeed returned to the skies, whence it came, I am convinced, not because he commanded mighty armies—for Cambyses also had mighty armies, and Cambyses was a mad-man who made successful use of his madness—but because he showed moderation and a sense of duty to a marvelous extent. I regard this trait in him as more admirable after his withdrawal from his native land than while he was defending her; for there was the alternative: Scipio should remain in Rome, or Rome should remain free. "It is my wish," said he, "not to infringe in the least upon our laws, or upon our customs, let all Roman citizens have equal rights. O my country, make the most of the good that I have done, but without me. I have been the cause of your freedom, and I shall also be its proof; I go into exile, if it is true that I have grown beyond what is to your advantage!"

2   What can I do but admire this magnanimity, which led him to withdraw into voluntary exile and to relieve the state of its burden? Matters had gone so far that either liberty must work harm to Scipio, or Scipio to liberty. Either of these things was wrong in the sight of heaven. So he gave way to the laws and withdrew to Liternum, thinking to make the state a debtor for his own exile no less than for the exile of Hannibal.

3   I have inspected the house, which is constructed of hewn stone; the wall which encloses a forest; the towers also, buttressed out on both sides for the purpose of defending the house; the well, concealed among buildings and shrubbery, large enough to keep a whole army supplied; and the small bath, buried in darkness according to the

old style, for our ancestors did not think that one could have a hot bath except in darkness. It was therefore a great pleasure to me to contrast Scipio's ways with our own. Think, in this tiny recess the "terror of Carthage," to whom Rome should offer thanks because she was not captured more than once, used to bathe a body wearied with work in the fields! For he was accustomed to keep himself busy and to cultivate the soil with his own hands, as the good old Romans were wont to do. Beneath this dingy roof he stood; and this floor, mean as it is, bore his weight.

4　But who in these days could bear to bathe in such a fashion? We think ourselves poor and mean if our walls are not resplendent with large and costly mirrors; if our marbles from Alexandria are not set off by mosaics of Numidian stone, if their borders are not faced over on all sides with difficult patterns, arranged in may colors like paintings; if our vaulted ceilings are not buried in glass; if our swimming-pools are not line with Thasian marble, once a rare and wonderful sight in any temple-pools into which we let down our bodies after they have been drained weak by abundant perspiration; and finally, if the water has not poured from silver spigots. I have so far been speaking of the ordinary bathing-establishments; what shall I say when I come to those of the freemen? What a vast number of statues, of columns that support nothing, but are built for decoration, merely in order to spend money! And what masses of water that fall crashing from level to level! We have become so luxurious that we will have nothing but precious stones to walk upon.

5　In this bath of Scipio's there are tiny chinks-you cannot call them windows-cut out of the stone wall in such a way as to admit light without weakening the fortifications; nowadays, however, people regard baths as fit only for moths if they have not been arranged that they receive the sun all day long through the widest of windows, if men cannot bathe and get a coat of tan at the same time, and if they cannot look out from their bath-tubs over stretches of land

and sea. So it goes; the establishments which had drawn crowds and had won admiration when thy were first opened are avoided and put back in the category of venerable antiques as soon as luxury has worked out some new device, to her own ultimate undoing. In the early days, however, there were few baths, and they were not fitted out with any display. For why should men elaborately fit out that which costs a penny only, and was invented for use, not merely for delight? The bathers of those days did not have water poured over them, nor did it always run fresh as if from a hot spring; and they did not believe that it mattered at all how perfectly pure was the water into which they were to leave their dirt. Ye gods, what a pleasure it is to enter that dark bath, covered with a common sort of roof, knowing that therein your hero Cato, as aedile, or Fabius Maximus, or one of the Cornelii, has warmed the water with his own hands! For this also used to be the duty of the noblest aediles—to enter these places to which the populace resorted, and to demand that they be cleaned and warmed to a heat required by considerations of use and health, not the heat that men have recently mad fashionable, as great as a conflagration—so much so, indeed, that a slave condemned for some criminal offence now ought to be bathed alive! It seems to me that nowadays there is no difference between "the bath is on fire," and 'the bath is warm."

6   How some persons nowadays condemn Scipio as a boor because he did not let daylight into his perspiring-room through wide windows, or because he did not roast in the strong sunlight and dawdle about until he could stew in the hot water! "Poor fool," they say, "he did not know how to live! He did not bathe in filtered water; it was often turbid, and after heavy rains almost muddy!" But it did not matter much to Scipio if he had to bathe in that way; he went there to wash off sweat, not ointment. And how do you suppose certain persons will answer me? They will say: "I don't envy Scipio; that was truly an exile's life-to put up with baths like those!" Friend, if you were wiser, you would know that Scipio did not

bathe every day. It is stated by those who have reported to us the old-time ways of Rome that the Romans washed only their arms and legs daily-because those were the members which gathered dirt in their daily toil-and bathed all over only once a week. Here someone will retort: "Yes; pretty dirty fellows they evidently were! How they mist have smelled!" But they smelled of the camp, the farm, and heroism. Now that spick- and-span bathing establishments have been devised, men are really fouler than of yore. What says Horatius Flaccus, when he wishes to describe a scoundrel, one who is notorious for his extreme luxury? He says: "Buccillus smells of perfume." Show me a Buccillus in these days; his smell would be the veritable goat-smell-he would take the place of the Gargonius with whom Horace in the same passage contrasted him. It is nowadays not enough to use ointment, unless you put on a fresh coat two or three times a day, to keep it from evaporating on the body. But why should a man boast of this perfume as if it were his own?

7   If what I am saying shall seem to you too pessimistic, charge it up against Scipio's country-house, where I have learned a lesson from Aegialus, a most careful householder and now the owner of this estate; he taught me that a tree can be transplanted, no matter how far gone in years. We old men must learn this precept; for there is none of us who is not planting an olive-yard for his successor. I have seen them bearing fruit in due season after three or four years of unproductiveness. And you too shall be shaded by the tree which "is slow to grow, but bringeth shade to cheer your grandsons in the far-off years," as our poet Vergil says.

8   Vergil sought, however, not what was nearest to the truth, but what was most appropriate, and aimed, not to teach the farmer, but to please the reader. For example, omitting all other errors of his, I will quote the passage in which it was incumbent upon me today to detect a fault: "In spring sow beans; then too, O clover plant, thou'rt welcomed by the crumbling furrows; and the millet calls for yearly care." You may judge by the following incident whether

those plants should be set out at the same time, or whether both should be sowed in the spring. It is June at the present writing, and we are well on towards July; and I have seen on this very day farmers harvesting beans and sowing millet....

9 I do not intend to tell you any more of these precepts, lest as Aegialus did with me, I may be training you up to be my competitor. Farewell.

» (63-65)

Some Arguments in Favor of the Simple Life

Lucius Annaeus Seneca

1 "I was shipwrecked before I got aboard." I shall not add how that happened, lest you may reckon this also as another of the Stoic paradoxes; and yet I shall, whenever you are willing to listen, nay, even though you be unwilling, prove to you that these words are by no means untrue, nor so surprising as one at first sight would think. Meantime, the journey showed me this: how easily we can make up our minds to do away with things whose loss, whenever it is necessary to part with them, we do not feel.

2 My friend Maximus and I have been spending a most happy period of two days, taking with us very few slaves—one carriage load—and no paraphernalia except what we wore on our persons. The mattress lies on the ground, and I upon the mattress. There are two rugs—one to spread beneath us and one to cover us. Nothing could have been subtracted from our luncheon; it took not more than an hour to prepare, and we were nowhere without dried figs, never without writing tablets. If I have bread, I used figs as a relish; if not, I regard figs as a substitute for bread. Hence they bring me a New Year feast every day, good thoughts and greatness of soul; for the soul is never greater than when it has laid aside all extraneous things, and has secured peace for itself by fearing nothing, and riches by craving no riches. The vehicle in which I have taken my seat is a farmer's cart. Only by walking do the mules show that they are alive. The driver is barefoot, and not because it is summer either. I can scarcely force myself to wish that others shall think this cart mine. My false embarrassment about the truth still holds out, you see; and whenever we meet a more sumptuous party I blush in spite of myself—proof that this conduct which I approve and applaud has not yet gained a firm and steadfast dwelling-place

within me. He who blushes at riding in a rattle-trap will boast when he rides in style. So my progress is still insufficient. I have not yet the courage openly to acknowledge my thriftiness. Even yet I am bothered by what other travelers think of me. But instead of this, I should really have uttered an opinion counter to that in which mankind believe, saying, "You are mad, you are misled, your admiration devotes itself to superfluous things! You estimate no man at his real worth. When property is concerned, you reckon up in this way with most scrupulous calculation those to whom you shall lend either money or benefits; for by now you enter benefits also as payments in your ledger. You say: 'His estates are wide, but his debts are large.' 'He has a fine house, but he has built it on borrowed capital.' 'No man will display a more brilliant retinue on short notice, but he cannot meet his debts.' 'If he pays off his creditors, he will have nothing left.'" So you will feel bound to do in all other cases as well,—to find out by elimination the amount of every man's actual possessions.

3   I suppose you call a man rich just because his gold plate goes with him even on his travels. because he farms land in all the provinces, because he unrolls a large account-book, because he owns estates near the city so great that men would grudge his holding them in the waste lands of Apulia. But after you have mentioned all these facts, he is poor. And why? He is in debt. "To what extent?" you ask. For all that he has. Or perchance you think it matters whether one has borrowed from another man or from Fortune. What good is there in mules caparisoned in uniform livery? Or in decorated chariots and

> Steeds decked with purple and with tapestry,
> With golden harness hanging from their necks,
> Champing their yellow bits, all clothed in gold?
> Neither master nor mule is improved by such trappings.

4   Marcus Cato the Censor, whose existence helped the state as much as die Scipio's—for while Scipio fought against our enemies, Cato

fought against bad morals,—used to ride a donkey, and a donkey, at that, which carried saddle-bags containing the master's necessaries. O how I should love to see him meet today on the road one of our coxcombs, with his outriders and Numidians, and a great cloud of dust before him! Your dandy would no doubt seem refined and well-attended in comparison with Marcus Cato,—your dandy, who, in the midst of all his luxurious paraphernalia, is chiefly concerned whether to turn his hand to the sword or to the hunting knife. O what a glory to the times in which he lived, for a general who had celebrated a triumph, a censor, and what is most noteworthy of all, a Cato, to be content with a single nag, and with less than a whole nag at that! For part of the animal was preempted by the baggage that hung down on either flank. Would you not therefore prefer Cato's steed, that single steed, saddle-worn by Cato himself, to the coxcomb's whole retinue of plump ponies, Spanish cobs, and trotters? I see that there will be no end in dealing with such a theme unless I make an end myself. So I shall now become silent, at least with reference to superfluous things like these; doubtless the man who first called them "hindrances" had a prophetic inkling that they would be the very sort of thing they now are. At present I should like to deliver to you the syllogisms, as yet very few, belonging to our school and bearing upon the question of virtue, which, in our opinion, is sufficient for the happy life.

5   "That which is good makes men good. For example, that which is good in the art of music makes the musician. But chance events do not make a good man; therefore, chance events are not goods." The Peripatetics reply to this by saying that the premise is false; that men do not in every case become good by means of that which is good; that in music there is something good, like a flute, a harp, or an organ suited to accompany singing; but that none of these instruments makes the musician. We shall then reply: "You do not understand in what sense we have used the phrase 'that which is good in music.' For we do not mean that which equips

the musician, but that which makes the musician; you, however, are referring to the instruments of the art, and not to the art itself. If, however, anything in the art of music is good, that will in every case make the musician." And I should like to put this idea still more clearly. We define the good in the art of music in two ways: first, that by which the performance of the musician is assisted, and second, that by which his art is assisted. Now the musical instruments have to do with his performance,—such as flutes and organs and harps; but they do not have to do with the musician's art itself. For he is an artist even without them; he may perhaps be lacking in the ability to practice his art. But the good in man is not in the same way twofold; for the good of man and the good of life are the same.

6   "That which can fall to the lot of any man, no matter how base or despised he may be, is not a good. But wealth falls to the lot of the pander and the trainer of gladiators; therefore wealth is not a good." "Another wrong premise," they say, "for we notice that goods fall to the lot of the very lowest sort of men, not only in the scholar's art, but also in the art of healing or in the art of navigating." These arts, however, make no profession of greatness of soul; they do not rise to any heights nor do they frown upon what fortune may bring. It is virtue that uplifts man and places him superior to what mortals hold dear; virtue neither craves overmuch nor fears to excess that which is called good or that which is called bad. Chelidon, one of Cleopatra's eunuchs, possessed great wealth; and recently Natalis—a man whose tongue was a shameless as it was dirty, a man whose mouth used to perform the vilest offices—was the heir of many, and also made many his heirs. What then? Was it his money that made him unclean, or did he himself besmirch his money? Money tumbles into the hands of certain men as a shilling tumbles down a sewer. Virtue stands above all such things. It is appraised in coin of its own minting; and it deems none of these random wind-falls to be good. But medicine and navigation do

not forbid themselves and their followers to marvel at such things. One who is not a good man can nevertheless be a physician, or a pilot, or a scholar,—yes, just as well as he can be a cook! He to whose lot it falls to possess something which is not of a random sort, cannot be called a random sort of man; a person is of the same sort as that which he possesses. A strong-box is worth just what it holds; or rather, it is a mere accessory of that which it holds. Who ever sets any price upon a full purse except the price established by the count of the money deposited therein? This also applies to the owners of great estates: they are only accessories and incidentals to their possessions.

7 Why, then, is the wise man great? Because he has a great soul. Accordingly, it is true that that which falls to the lot even of the most despicable person is not a good. Thus, I should never regard inactivity as a good; for even the tree-frog and the flea possess this quality. Nor should I regard rest and freedom from trouble as a good; for what is more at leisure than a worm? Do you ask what it is that produces the wise man? That which produces a god. You must grant that the wise man has an element of godliness, heaven-liness, grandeur. The good does not come to every one, nor does it allow any random person to possess it. Behold:

> What fruits each country bears, or will not bear;
> Here corn, and there the vine grow richlier.
> And elsewhere still the tender tree and grass
> Unbidden clothe themselves in green. Seest thou
> How Tmolus ships its saffron perfumes forth,
> And ivory comes from Ind; soft Sheba sends
> Its incense, and the unclad Chalybes
> Their iron.

8 These products are apportioned to separate countries in order that human beings may be constrained to traffic among themselves, each seeking something from his neighbor in his turn. So the Supreme Good has also its own abode. It does not grow where ivory grows, or iron. Do you ask where the Supreme Good dwells?

In the soul. And unless the soul be pure and holy, there is no room in it for God.

9 "Good does not result from evil. But riches result from greed; therefore riches are not a good." "It is not true," they say, "that good does not result from evil. For money comes from sacrilege and theft. Accordingly, although sacrilege and theft are evil, yet they are evil only because they work more evil than good. For they bring gain; but the gain is accompanied by fear, anxiety, and torture of mind and body." Whoever says this must perforce admit that sacrilege, though it be an evil because it works much evil, is yet partly good because it accomplishes a certain amount of good. What can be more monstrous than this, We have, to be sure, actually convinced the world that sacrilege, theft, and adultery are to be regarded as among the goods. How many men there are who do not blush at theft, how many who boast of having committed adultery! For petty sacrilege is punished, but sacrilege on a grand scale is honored by a triumphal procession. Besides, sacrilege, if it is wholly good in some respect, will also be honorable and will be called right conduct; for it is conduct which concerns ourselves. But no human being, on a serious consideration, admits this idea.

10 Therefore, goods cannot spring from evil. For if, as you object, sacrilege is an evil for the single reason that it brings on much evil, if you but absolve sacrilege of its punishment and pledge it immunity, sacrilege will be wholly good. And yet the worse punishment for crimes lies in the crime itself. You are mistaken, I maintain, if you propose to reserve your punishments for the hangman or the prison; the crime is punished immediately after it is committed; nay, rather, at the moment when it is committed. Hence, good does not spring from evil, any more than figs grow from olive-trees. Things which grow correspond to their seed; and goods cannot depart from their class. As that which is honorable does not grow from that which is base, so neither does good grow from evil. For the honorable and the good are identical.

11 Certain of our school oppose this statement as follows: "Let us suppose that money taken from any source whatsoever is a good; even though it is taken by an act of sacrilege, the money does not on that account derive its origin from sacrilege. You may get my meaning through the following illustration: In the same jar there is a piece of gold and there is a serpent. If you take the gold from the jar, it is not just because the serpent is there too, I say, that the jar yields me the gold—because it contains the serpent as well,—but it yields the gold in spite of containing the serpent also. Similarly, gain results from sacrilege, not just because sacrilege is a base and accursed act, but because it contains gain also. As the serpent in the jar is an evil, and not the gold which lies there beside the serpent; so in an act of sacrilege it is the crime, not the profit, that is evil." But I differ from these men; for the conditions in each case are not at all the same. In the one instance I can take the gold without the serpent, in the other I cannot make the profit without committing the sacrilege. The gain in the latter case does not lie side by side with the crime; it is blended with the crime.

12 "That which, while we are desiring to attain it, involves us in many evils, is not a good. But while we are desiring to attain riches, we become involved in many evils; therefore, riches are not a good." "Your first premise," they say, "contains two meanings; one is: we become involved in many evils while we are desiring to attain riches. But we also become involved in many evils while we are desiring to attain virtue. One man, while traveling in order to prosecute his studies, suffers shipwreck, and another is taken captive. The second meaning is as follows: that through which we become involved in evils is not a good. And it will not logically follow from our proposition that we become involved in evils through riches or through pleasure; otherwise, if it is through riches that we become involved in many evils, riches are not only not a good, but they are positively an evil. You, however, maintain merely that they are not a good. Moreover," the objector says, "you grant that riches are of some use. You reckon them among the advantages: and yet on this basis they cannot even be an advantage, for it is through the pursuit of riches that we suffer much disadvantage." Certain men answer this objection as follows: "You are mistaken if you ascribe disadvantages to riches. Riches injure no one; it is a man's own folly, or his neighbor's wickedness, that harms him in each case, just as a sword by itself does not slay; it is merely the weapon used by the slayer. Riches themselves do not harm you, just because it is merely the weapon used by the slayer. Riches themselves do not harm you, just because it is on account of riches that you suffer harm."

13 I think that the reasoning of Posidonius is better: he holds that riches are a cause of evil, not because, of themselves, they do any evil, but because they goad men on so that they are ready to do evil. For the efficient cause, which necessarily produces harm at once, is one thing, and the antecedent cause is another. It is this antecedent cause which inheres in riches; they puff up the spirit and beget pride, they bring on unpopularity and unsettle the mind to such an extent that the mere reputation of having wealth, though it is bound to harm us, nevertheless affords delight. All goods, however, ought properly to be free from blame; they are pure, they do not corrupt the spirit, and they do not tempt us. They do indeed, uplift and broaden the spirit, but without puffing it up. Those things which are goods produce confidence, but riches produce shamelessness. The things which are goods give us greatness of soul, but riches give us arrogance. And arrogance is nothing else than a false show of greatness.

14 "According to that argument," the objector says, 'riches are not only not a good, but are a positive evil.' Now they would be an evil if they did harm of themselves, and if as I remarked, it were the efficient cause which inheres in them; in fact, however, it is the antecedent cause which inheres in riches, and indeed it is that cause which, so far from merely arousing the spirit, actually drags it along by force. Yes, riches shower upon us a semblance of the

good, which is like the reality and wins credence in the eyes of many men. the antecedent cause inheres in virtue also, it is this which brings on envy—for many men become unpopular because of their wisdom, and many men because of their justice. But this cause, though it inheres in virtue, is not the result of virtue itself, nor is it a mere semblance of the reality: nay on the contrary, far more like the reality is that vision which is flashed by virtue upon the spirits of men, summoning them to love it and marvel thereat.

15 Posidonius thinks that the syllogism should be framed a follows: "Things which bestow upon the soul no greatness or confidence or freedom from care are not goods. But riches and health and similar conditions do none of these things; therefore, riches and health are not goods." This syllogism he then goes on to extend still further in the following way: "Things which bestow upon the soul no greatness or confidence or freedom from care, but on the other hand create in it arrogance, vanity, and insolence, are evils. But things which are the gift of Fortune drive us into these evil ways. Therefore these things are not goods." "But," says the objector, "by such reasoning, things which are the gift of Fortune will not even be advantages." No, advantages and goods stand each in a different situation. An advantage is that which contains more of usefulness than of annoyance. But a good to be unmixed and with no element in it of harmfulness. A thing is not good if it contains more benefit. Besides, advantages may be predicated of animals, of men who are less than perfect, and of fools. Hence the advantageous may have an element of disadvantage mingled with it, but the word "advantageous" is used of the compound because it is judged by its predominant element. The good, however, can be predicated of the wise man alone; it is bound to be without alloy.

16 Be a good cheer; there is only one knot left for you to untangle, though it is a knot for a Hercules: "Good does not result from evil. But riches result from numerous cases of poverty; therefore, riches are not a good." This syllogism is not recognized by our school,

but the Peripatetics both concoct it and give its solution. Posidonius, however, remarks that this fallacy, which has been bandied about among all the schools of dialectic, is refuted by Antipater as follows: "The work 'Poverty' is used to denote, not the possession of something, but the non-possession or, as the ancients have put it deprivation, (for the Greeks use the phrase 'by deprivation,' meaning 'negatively'). 'Poverty' states not what a man has, but what he has not. Consequently there can be no fullness resulting from a multitude of voids; many positive things, and many deficiencies, make up riches. You have," says he, "a wrong notion of the meaning of what poverty is. For poverty does not mean the possession of little, but the non-possession of much; it is used, therefore, not of what a man has, but of what he lacks. "I could express my meaning more easily if there were a Latin word which could translate the Greek word which means "not-possessing." Antipater assigns this quality too poverty, but for my part I cannot see what else poverty is than the possession of little. If ever we have plenty of leisure, we shall investigate the question; What is the essence of riches, and what the essence of poverty; but when the time comes, we shall also consider whether it is not better to try to mitigate poverty, and to relieve wealth of its arrogance, than to quibble about the words as if the question of the things were already decided.

17 Let us suppose that we have been summoned to an assembly; an act dealing with the abolition of riches has been brought before the meeting. Shall we be supporting it, or opposing it, if we use these syllogisms? Will these syllogisms help us to bring it about that the Roman people shall demand poverty and praise it—poverty, the foundation and cause of their empire,—and, on the other hand, shall shrink in fear from their present wealth, reflecting that they have found it among the victims of their conquests, that wealth is the source from which office-seeking and bribery and disorder have burst into a city once characterized by the utmost scrupulousness and sobriety, and that because of wealth an exhibition all too lavish

is made of the spoils of conquered nations; reflecting, finally, that whatever one people has snatched away from all the rest may still more easily be snatched by all away from one? Nay, it were better to support this law by our conduct and to subdue our desires by direct assault rather than to circumvent them by logic. If we can, let us speak more boldly; if not, let us speak more frankly.

»   (63-65)

On the Healing Power of the Mind

Lucius Annaeus Seneca

1 That you are frequently troubled by the snuffling of catarrh and by short attacks of fever which follow after long and chronic catarrhal seizures, I am sorry to hear; particularly because I have experienced this sort of illness myself, and scorned it in its early stages. For when I was still young, I could put up with hardships and show a bold front to illness. But I finally succumbed, and arrived at such state that I could do nothing but snuffle, reduced as I was to the extremity of thinness. I often entertained the impulse of ending my life then and there; but the thought of my kind old father kept me back. For I reflected, not how bravely I had the power to die, but how little power he had to bear bravely the loss of me. And so I commanded myself to live. For sometimes it is an act of bravery even to live.

2 Now I shall tell you what consoled me during those days, stating at the outset that these very aids to my peace of mind were as efficacious as medicine. Honorable consolation results in a cure; and whatever has uplifted the soul helps the body also. My studies were my salvation. I place it to the credit of philosophy that I recovered and regained my strength. I owe my life to philosophy, and that is the least of my obligations! My friends, too, helped me greatly toward good health; I used to be comforted by their cheering words, by the hours they spent at my bedside, and by their conversation. Nothing, my excellent Lucilius, refreshes and aids a sick man so much as the affection of his friends; nothing so steals away the expectation and the fear of death. In fact, I could not believe that, if they survived me, I should be dying at all. Yes, I repeat, it seemed to me that I should continue to live, not with them, but through them. I imagined myself not to be yielding up my soul, but to be making it over to them.

3 All these things gave me the inclination to succor myself and to endure any torture; besides, it is a most miserable state to have lost one's zest for dying, and to have no zest for living. These, then, are the remedies to which you should have recourse. The physician will prescribe your walks and your exercise; he will warn you not to become addicted to idleness, as is the tendency of the inactive invalid; he will order you to read in a louder voice and to exercise your lungs, the passages and cavity of which are affected; or to sail and shake up your bowels by a little mild emotion; he will recommend the proper food, and the suitable time for aiding your strength with wine or refraining from it in order to keep your cough from being irritated and hacking. But as for me, my counsel to you is this,—and it is a cure, not merely of this disease of yours, but of your whole life,—"Despise death." There is no sorrow in the world, when we have escaped form the fear of death. There are these three serious elements in every disease: fear of death, bodily pain, and interruption of pleasures. Concerning death enough has been said, and I shall add only a word: this fear is not a fear of disease, but a fear of nature. Disease has often postponed death, and a vision of dying has been many a man's salvation. You will die, not because you are ill, but because you are alive; even when you have been cured, the same end awaits you; when you have recovered, it will be not death, but ill-death, that you have escaped. Let us now return to the consideration of the characteristic disadvantages of disease: it is accompanied by great suffering. The suffering, however, is rendered endurable by interruptions; for the strain of extreme pain must come to an end. No man can suffer both severely and for a long time; Nature, who loves us most tenderly, has so constituted us as to make pain either endurable or short. The severest pains have their seat in the most slender part of our body; nerves, joints, and any other of the narrow passages, hurt most cruelly when they have developed trouble within their contracted spaces. But these parts soon become numb, and by reason of the pain itself lose the sensation of pain, whether because the life-force, when checked

in its natural course and changed for the worse, loses the peculiar power through which it thrives and through which it warns us, or because the diseased humors of the body, when they cease to have a place into which they may flow, are thrown back upon themselves, and deprive of sensation the parts where they have caused congestion. So ought, both in the feet and in the hands, and all pain in the vertebrae and in the nerves, have their intervals of the rest at the times when they have dulled the parts which they before had tortured; the first twinges, in all such cases, are what cause the distress, and their onset is checked by lapse of time, so that there is an end of pain when numbness has set in. Pain in the teeth, eyes. And ears is most acute for the very reason that it begins among the narrow spaces of the body,—no less acute, indeed, than in the head it self. But if it is more violent than usual, it turns to delirium and stupor. This is, accordingly, a consolation for excessive pain,—that you cannot help ceasing to feel it if you feel it to excess. The reason, however, why the inexperienced are impatient when their bodies suffer is, that they have not accustomed themselves to be contented in spirit. They have been closely associated with the body. Therefore a high-minded and sensible man divorces soul from body, and dwells much with the better or divine part, and only as far as he must with this complaining and frail portion.

4   "But it is a hardship," men say, "to do without our customary pleasures,—to fast, to feel thirst and hunger." These are indeed serious when one first abstains from them. Later the desire dies down, because the appetites themselves which lead to desire are wearied and forsake us; then the stomach becomes petulant, then the food which we craved before becomes hateful. Our very wants die away. But there is no bitterness in doing without that which you have ceased to desire. Moreover, every pain sometimes stops, or at any rate slackens; moreover, one may take precautions against its return, and, when it threatens, may check it by means of remedies. Every variety of pain has its premonitory symptoms; this is true,

at any rate, of pain that is habitual and recurrent. One can endure the suffering which disease entails, if one has come to regard its results with scorn. But do not of your own accord make your troubles heavier to bear and burden yourself with complaining. Pain is slight if opinion has added nothing to it; but if, on the other hand, you begin to encourage yourself and say, "It is nothing,—a trifling matter at most; keep a stout heart and it will soon cease"; then in thinking it slight, you will make it slight. Everything depends on opinion; ambition, luxury, greed, hark back to opinion. It is according to opinion that we suffer. A man is as wretched as he has convinced himself that he is. I hold that we should do away with complaint about past sufferings and with all language like this: "None has ever been worse off than I. What sufferings, what evils have I endured! No one has thought that I shall recover. How often have my family bewailed me, and the physicians given me over! Men who are placed on the rack are not torn asunder with such agony!" However, even if all this is true, it is over and gone. What benefit is there in reviewing past sufferings, and in being unhappy, just because once you were unhappy? Besides, every one adds much to his own ills, and tells lies to himself. And that which was bitter to bear is pleasant to have borne; it is natural to rejoice at the ending of one's ills.

5   Two elements must therefore be rooted out once for all,—the fear of future suffering, and the recollection of past suffering, since the latter no longer concerns me, and the former concerns me not yet. But when set in the very midst of troubles one should say: "Perchance some day the memory of his sorrow / Will even bring delight." Let such man fight against them with all his might: if he once gives way, he will be vanquished; but if he strives against his sufferings, he will conquer. As it is, however, what most men do is to drag down upon their own heads a falling ruin which they ought to try to support. If you begin to withdraw your support from that which thrusts toward you and totters and is ready to

plunge, it will follow you and lean more heavily upon you; but if you hold your ground and make up your mind to push against it, it will be forced back. What blows do athletes receive on their faces and all over their bodies! Nevertheless, through their desire for fame they endure every torture, and they undergo these things not only because they are fighting but in order to be able to fight. Their very training means torture. So let us also win the way to victory in all our struggles,-for the reward is not a garland or a palm or a trumpeter who calls for silence at the proclamation of our names, but rather virtue, steadfastness of soul, and a peace that is won for all time, if fortune has once been utterly vanquished in any combat. You say, "I feel severe pain." What then; are you relieved from feeling it, if you endure it like a woman? Just as an enemy is more dangerous to a retreating army, so every trouble that fortune brings attacks us all the harder if we yield and turn our backs. "But the trouble is serious." What? Is it for this purpose that we are strong,-that we may have light burdens to bear? Would you have your illness long- drawn-out, or would you have it quick and short? If it is long, it means a respite, allows you a period for resting yourself, bestows upon you the boon of time in plenty; as it arises, so it must also subside. A short and rapid illness will do one of two things: it will quench or be quenched. And what difference does it make whether it is not or I am not? In either case there is an end of pain.

6 This, too, will help-to turn the mind aside to thoughts of other things and thus to depart from pain. Call to mind what honorable or brave deeds you have done; consider the good side of your own life. Run over in your memory those things which you have particularly admired. Then think of all the brave men who have conquered pain: of him who continued to read his book as he allowed the cutting out of varicose veins; of him who did not cease to smile, though that very smile so enraged his torturers that they tried upon him every instrument of their cruelty. If pain can be conquered by

a smile, will it not be conquered by reason? You may tell me now of whatever you like-of colds, hard coughing-spells that bring up parts of our entrails, fever that parches our very vitals, thirst, limbs so twisted that the joints protrude in different directions; yet worse than these are the stake, the rack, the red-hot plates, the instrument that reopens wounds while the wounds themselves are still swollen and that drives their imprint still deeper. Nevertheless there have been men who have not uttered a moan amid these tortures. "More yet!" says the torturer; but the victim has not begged for release. "More yet!" he says again; but no answer has come. "More yet!" the victim has smiled, and heartily, too. Can you not bring yourself, after an example like this, to make a mock at pain?

7 "But," you object, "my illness does not allow me to be doing anything; it has withdrawn me from all my duties." It is your body that is hampered by ill-health, and not your soul as well. It is for this reason that it clogs the feet of the runner and will hinder the handiwork of the cobbler or the artisan; but if your soul be habitually in practice, you will plead and teach, listen and learn, investigate and meditate. What more is necessary? Do you think that you are doing nothing if you possess self-control in your illness? You will be showing that a disease can be overcome, or at any rate endured. There is, I assure you, a place for virtue even upon a bed of sickness. It is not only the sword and the battle-line that prove the soul alert and unconquered by fear; a man can display bravery even when wrapped in his bed-clothes. You have something to do: wrestle bravely with disease. If it shall compel you to nothing, beguile you to nothing, it is a notable example that you display. O what ample matter were there for renown, if we could have spectators of our sickness! Be your own spectator; seek your own applause.

8 Again, there are two kinds of pleasures. Disease checks the pleasures of the body, but does not do away with them. Nay, if the truth is to be considered, it serves to excite them; for the thirstier a man is, the more he enjoys a drink; the hungrier he is, the more pleasure he

takes in food. Whatever falls to one's lot after a period of abstinence is welcomed with great zest. The other kind, however, the pleasures of the mind, which are higher and less uncertain, no physician can refuse to the sick man. Whoever seeks these and knows well what they are, scorns all the blandishments of the senses. Men say, "Poor sick fellow!" But why? Is it because it he does not mix snow with his wine, or because he does not revive the chill of his drink-mixed as it is in a good- sized bowl-by chipping ice into it? Or because he does not have Lucrine oysters opened fresh at his table? Or because there is no din of cooks about his dining-hall, as they bring in their very cooking apparatus along with their viands? For luxury has already devised this fashion-of having the kitchen accompany the dinner, so that food may not grow luke-warm, or fail to be hot enough for a palate which has already become hardened. "Poor sick fellow!"-he will eat as much as he can digest. There will be no boar lying before his eyes, banished from the table as if it were a common meat; and on his sideboard there will be heaped together no breast- meat of birds, because it sickens him to see birds served whole. But what evil has been done to you? You will dine like a sick man, nay, some-times like a sound man.

9 All these things, however, can be easily endured-gruel, warm water, and anything else that seems insupportable to a fastidious man, to one who is wallowing in luxury, sick in soul rather than in body-if only we cease to shudder at death. And we shall cease, if once we have gained a knowledge of the limits of good and evil; then, and then only, life will not weary us, neither will death make us afraid. For surfeit of self can never seize upon a life that surveys all the things which are manifold, great, divine; only idle leisure is wont to make men hate their lives. To one who roams through the universe, the truth can pall; it will be the untruths that will cloy. And, on the other hand, if death comes near with its summons, even though it be untimely in its arrival, though it cut one off in one's prime, a man has had a taste of all that the longest life can give. Such a man

has in great measure to understand the universe. He knows that honorable things do not depend on time for their growth; but any life must seem short to those who measure its length by pleasures which are empty and for that reason unbounded.

10 Refresh yourself with such thoughts as these, and meanwhile reserve some hours for our letters. There will come a time when we shall be united again and brought together; however short this time may be, we shall make it long by knowing how to employ it. For, as Posidonius says: "A single day among the learned lasts longer than the longest life among the ignorant." Meanwhile, hold fast to this thought, and grip it close: yield not to adversity; trust not to prosperity; keep before your eyes the full scope of Fortune's power, as if she would surely do whatever is in her power to do. That which has been long expected comes more gently. Farewell.

» (63–65)

A Penny Plain and Twopence Coloured

Robert Louis Stevenson

1   These words will be familiar to all students of Skelt's Juvenile Drama. That national monument, after having changed its name to Park's, to Webb's, to Redington's, and last of all to Pollock's, has now become, for the most part, a memory. Some of its pillars, like Stonehenge, are still afoot, the rest clean vanished. In may be the Museum numbers a full set; and Mr. Ionides perhaps, or else her gracious Majesty, may boast their great collections; but to the plain private person they are become, like Raphaels, unattainable. I have, at different times, possessed Aladdin, The Red Rover, The Blind Boy, The Old Oak Chest, The Wood Dæmon, Jack Sheppard, The Miller and his Men, Der Freischütz, The Smuggler, The Forest of Bondy, Robin Hood, The Waterman, Richard I., My Poll and my Partner Joe, The Inchcape Bell (imperfect), and Three-Fingered Jack, The Terror of Jamaica; and I have assisted others in the illumination of The Maid of the Inn and The Battle of Waterloo. In this roll-call of stirring names you read the evidences of a happy childhood; and though not half of them are still to be procured of any living stationer, in the mind of their once happy owner all survive, kaleidoscopes of changing pictures, echoes of the past.

2   There stands, I fancy, to this day (but now how fallen!) a certain stationer's shop at a corner of the wide thoroughfare that joins the city of my childhood with the sea. When, upon any Saturday, we made a party to behold the 117 ships, we passed that corner; and since in those days I loved a ship as a man loves Burgundy or daybreak, this of itself had been enough to hallow it. But there was more than that. In the Leith Walk window, all the year round, there stood displayed a theatre in working order, with a "forest set," a "combat," and a few "robbers carousing" in the slides; and

below and about, dearer tenfold to me! the plays themselves, those budgets of romance, lay tumbled one upon another. Long and often have I lingered there with empty pockets. One figure, we shall say, was visible in the first plate of characters, bearded, pistol in hand, or drawing to his ear the clothyard arrow; I would spell the name: was it Macaire, or Long Tom Coffin, or Grindoff, 2d dress? O, how I would long to see the rest! how—if the name by chance were hidden—I would wonder in what play he figured, and what immortal legend justified his attitude and strange apparel! And then to go within, to announce yourself as an intending purchaser, and, closely watched, be suffered to undo those bundles and breathlessly devour those pages of gesticulating villains, epileptic combats, bosky forests, palaces and war-ships, frowning fortresses and prison vaults—it was a giddy joy. That shop, which was dark and smelt of Bibles, was a loadstone rock for all that bore the name of boy. They could not pass it by, nor, having entered, leave it. It was a place besieged; the shopmen, like the Jews rebuilding Salem, had a double task. They kept us at the stick's end, frowned us down, snatched each play out of our hand ere we were trusted with another; and, incredible as it may sound, used to demand of us upon our entrance, like banditti, if we came with money or with empty hand. Old Mr. Smith himself, worn out with my eternal vacillation, once swept the treasures from before me, with the cry: "I do not believe, child, that you are an intending purchaser at all!" These were the dragons of the garden; but for such joys of paradise we could have faced the Terror of Jamaica himself. Every sheet we fingered was 118 another lightning glance into obscure, delicious story; it was like wallowing in the raw stuff of story-books. I know nothing to compare with it save now and then in dreams, when I am privileged to read in certain unwrit stories of adventure, from which I awake to find the world all vanity. The crux of Buridan's donkey was as nothing to the uncertainty of the boy as he handled and lingered and doated on these bundles of delight; there was a physical pleasure in the sight and touch of them which he would jealously prolong; and when at length the deed was done, the play selected, and the impatient shopman had brushed the rest into the grey portfolio, and the boy was forth again, a little late for dinner, the lamps springing into light in the blue winter's even, and The Miller, or The Rover, or some kindred drama clutched against his side—on what gay feet he ran, and how he laughed aloud in exultation! I can hear that laughter still. Out of all the years of my life, I can recall but one home-coming to compare with these, and that was on the night when I brought back with me the "Arabian Entertainments" in the fat, old, double-columned volume with the prints. I was just well into the story of the Hunchback, I remember, when my clergyman-grandfather (a man we counted pretty stiff) came in behind me. I grew blind with terror. But instead of ordering the book away, he said he envied me. Ah, well he might!

3   The purchase and the first half-hour at home, that was the summit. Thenceforth the interest declined by little and little. The fable, as set forth in the playbook, proved to be unworthy of the scenes and characters: what fable would not? Such passages as: "Scene 6. The Hermitage. Night set scene. Place back of scene 1, No. 2, at back of stage and hermitage, Fig. 2, out of set piece, R. H. in a slanting direction"—such passages, I say, though very practical, are hardly to be called good reading. Indeed, as literature, these dramas did not much appeal to me. I forget the very outline of the plots. Of The Blind 119Boy, beyond the fact that he was a most injured prince, and once, I think, abducted, I know nothing. And The Old Oak Chest, what was it all about? that proscript (1st dress), that prodigious number of banditti, that old woman with the broom, and the magnificent kitchen in the third act (was it in the third?)—they are all fallen in a deliquium, swim faintly in my brain, and mix and vanish.

4   I cannot deny that joy attended the illumination; nor can I quite forgive that child who, wilfully foregoing pleasure, stoops to "twopence coloured." With crimson lake (hark to the sound

of it—crimson lake!—the horns of elf-land are not richer on the ear)—with crimson lake and Prussian blue a certain purple is to be compounded which, for cloaks especially, Titian could not equal. The latter colour with gamboge, a hated name although an exquisite pigment, supplied a green of such a savoury greenness that to-day my heart regrets it. Nor can I recall without a tender weakness the very aspect of the water where I dipped my brush. Yes, there was pleasure in the painting. But when all was painted, it is needless to deny it, all was spoiled. You might, indeed, set up a scene or two to look at; but to cut the figures out was simply sacrilege; nor could any child twice court the tedium, the worry, and the long-drawn disenchantment of an actual performance. Two days after the purchase the honey had been sucked. Parents used to complain; they thought I wearied of my play. It was not so: no more than a person can be said to have wearied of his dinner when he leaves the bones and dishes; I had got the marrow of it and said grace.

5   Then was the time to turn to the back of the playbook and to study that enticing double file of names where poetry, for the true child of Skelt, reigned happy and glorious like her Majesty the Queen. Much as I have travelled in these realms of gold, I have yet seen, upon that map or abstract, names of El Dorados that still haunt the ear of memory, and are still but names. The 120Floating Beacon—why was that denied me? or The Wreck Ashore? Sixteen-String Jack, whom I did not even guess to be a highwayman, troubled me awake and haunted my slumbers; and there is one sequence of three from that enchanted calendar that I still at times recall, liked a loved verse of poetry: Lodoiska, Silver Palace, Echo of Westminster Bridge. Names, bare names, are surely more to children than we poor, grown-up, obliterated fools remember.

6   The name of Skelt itself has always seemed a part and parcel of the charm of his productions. It may be different with the rose, but the attraction of this paper drama sensibly declined when Webb had crept into the rubric: a poor cuckoo, flaunting in Skelt's nest.

And now we have reached Pollock, sounding deeper gulfs. Indeed, this name of Skelt appears so stagey and piratic, that I will adopt it boldly to design these qualities. Skeltery, then, is a quality of much art. It is even to be found, with reverence be it said, among the works of nature. The stagey is its generic name; but it is an old, insular, home-bred staginess; not French, domestically British; not of to-day, but smacking of O. Smith, Fitzball, and the great age of melodrama; a peculiar fragrance haunting it; uttering its unimportant message in a tone of voice that has the charm of fresh antiquity. I will not insist upon the art of Skelt's purveyors. These wonderful characters that once so thrilled our soul with their bold attitude, array of deadly engines and incomparable costume, to-day look somewhat pallidly; the extreme hard favour of the heroine strikes me, I had almost said with pain; the villain's scowl no longer thrills me like a trumpet; and the scenes themselves, those once unparalleled landscapes, seem the efforts of a prentice hand. So much of fault we find; but on the other side the impartial critic rejoices to remark the presence of a great unity of gusto; of those direct clap-trap appeals, which a man is dead and buriable when he fails to answer; of the footlight glamour, the ready-made, bare-faced, transpontine picturesque, a thing not one with cold reality, but how much dearer to the mind!

7 The scenery of Skeltdom—or, shall we say, the kingdom of Transpontus?—had a prevailing character. Whether it set forth Poland as in The Blind Boy, or Bohemia with The Miller and his Men, or Italy with The Old Oak Chest, still it was Transpontus. A botanist could tell it by the plants. The hollyhock was all-pervasive, running wild in deserts; the dock was common, and the bending reed; and overshadowing these were poplar, palm, potato tree, and Quercus Skeltica—brave growths. The graves were all embowelled in the Surrey-side formation; the soil was all betrodden by the light pump of T. P. Cooke. Skelt, to be sure, had yet another, an Oriental string: he held the gorgeous East in fee; and in the new quarter

of Hyères, say, in the garden of the Hôtel des Îles d'Or, you may behold these blessed visions realised. But on these I will not dwell; they were an outwork; it was in the Occidental scenery that Skelt was all himself. It had a strong flavour of England; it was a sort of indigestion of England and drop-scenes, and I am bound to say was charming. How the roads wander, how the castle sits upon the hill, how the sun eradiates from behind the cloud, and how the congregated clouds themselves uproll, as stiff as bolsters! Here is the cottage interior, the usual first flat, with the cloak upon the nail, the rosaries of onions, the gun and powder-horn and corner-cupboard; here is the inn (this drama must be nautical, I foresee Captain Luff and Bold Bob Bowsprit) with the red curtain, pipes, spittoons, and eight-day clock; and there again is that impressive dungeon with the chains, which was so dull to colour. England, the hedgerow elms, the thin brick houses, windmills, glimpses of the navigable Thames—England, when at last I came to visit it, was only Skelt made evident: to cross the border was, for the Scotsman, to come home to Skelt; there was the inn-sign and there the horse-trough, all foreshadowed in the faithful Skelt. If, at the ripe age of 122 fourteen years, I bought a certain cudgel, got a friend to load it, and thenceforward walked the tame ways of the earth my own ideal, radiating pure romance—still I was but a puppet in the hand of Skelt; the original of that regretted bludgeon, and surely the antitype of all the bludgeon kind, greatly improved from Cruikshank, had adorned the hand of Jonathan Wild, pl. 1. "This is mastering me," as Whitman cries, upon some lesser provocation. What am I? what are life, art, letters, the world, but what my Skelt has made them? He stamped himself upon my immaturity. The world was plain before I knew him, a poor penny world; but soon it was all coloured with romance. If I go to the theatre to see a good old melodrama, 'tis but Skelt a little faded. If I visit a bold scene in nature, Skelt would have been bolder; there had been certainly a castle on that mountain, and the hollow tree—that set-piece—I seem to miss it in the foreground. Indeed, out of this cut-and-dry, dull, swaggering, obtrusive and infantile art, I seem to have learned the very spirit of my life's enjoyment; met there the shadows of the characters I was to read about and love in a late future; got the romance of Der Freischütz long ere I was to hear of Weber or the mighty Formes; acquired a gallery of scenes and characters with which, in the silent theatre of the brain, I might enact all novels and romances; and took from these rude cuts an enduring and transforming pleasure. Reader—and yourself?

8   A word of moral: it appears that B. Pollock, late J. Redington, No. 73 Hoxton Street, not only publishes twenty-three of these old stage favourites, but owns the necessary plates and displays a modest readiness to issue other thirty-three. If you love art, folly, or the bright eyes of children, speed to Pollock's or to Clarke's of Garrick Street. In Pollock's list of publicanda I perceive a pair of my ancient aspirations: The Wreck Ashore and Sixteen-String Jack; and I cherish the belief that when these shall see once more the light of day, B. Pollock will 123 remember this apologist. But, indeed, I have a dream at times that is not all a dream. I seem to myself to wander in a ghostly street—E.W., I think, the postal district—close below the fool's cap of St. Paul's, and yet within easy hearing of the echo of the Abbey Bridge. There in a dim shop, low in the roof and smelling strong of glue and footlights, I find myself in quaking treaty with great Skelt himself, the aboriginal, all dusty from the tomb. I buy, with what a choking heart—I buy them all, all but the pantomimes; I pay my mental money, and go forth; and lo! the packets are dust.

»   (1884)

The Ruins

H. M. Tomlinson

1   For more than two years this town could not have been more remote from us if it had been in another planet. We were but a few miles from it, but the hills hid it, and the enemy was between us and the hills. This town was but a name, a legend.

2   Now the enemy had left it. When going into it for the first time you had the feeling that either you or the town was bewitched. Were you really there? Were time and space abolished? Or perhaps the town itself was supernatural; it was spectral, projected by unknowable evil. And for what purpose? Suspicious of its silence, of its solitude, of all its aspects, you verified its stones by touching them, and looked about for signs that men had once been there.

3   Such a town, which has long been in the zone of fire, and is then uncovered by the foe, gives a wayfarer who early ventures into it the feeling that this is the day after the Last Day, and that he has been overlooked. Somehow he did not hear Gabriel's trumpet; everybody else has gone on. There is not a sound but the subdued crackling of flames hidden somewhere in the overthrown and abandoned. There is no movement but where faint smoke is wreathing slowly across the deserted streets. The unexpected collapse of a wall or cornice is frightful. So is the silence which follows. A starved kitten, which shapes out of nothing and is there complete and instantaneous at your feet—ginger stripes, and a mew which is weak, but a veritable voice of the living—is first a great surprise, and then a ridiculous comfort. It follows you about. When you miss it, you go back to look for it—to find the miserable object racing frantically to meet you. Lonely? The Poles are not more desolate. There is no place as forlorn as that where man once was established and busy, where the patient work of his hands is all round, but where silence has fallen like a secret so dense that you feel that if it were not also so desper-

ately invisible you could grasp a corner of it, lift the dark veil, and learn a little of what was the doom of those who have vanished. What happened to them?

4   It cannot be guessed. House fronts have collapsed in rubble across the road. There is a smell of opened vaults. All the homes are blind. Their eyes have been put out. Many of the buildings are without roofs, and their walls have come down to raw serrations. Slates and tiles have avalanched into the street, or the roof itself is entire, but has dropped sideways over the ruin below as a drunken cap over the dissolute. The lower floors are heaps of damp mortar and bricks. Very rarely a solitary picture hangs awry on the wall of a house where there is no other sign that it was ever inhabited. I saw in such a room the portrait of a child who in some moment long ago laughed while it clasped a dog in a garden. You continue to gaze at a sign like that, you don't know why, as though something you cannot name might be divined, if you could but hit upon the key to the spell. What is the name of the evil that has fallen on mankind?

5   The gardens beyond are to be seen through the thin and gaping walls of the streets, and there, overturned and defaced by shell-bursts and the crude subsoil thrown out from dug-outs, a few ragged shrubs survive. A rustic bower is lumbered with empty bottles, meat tins, a bird-cage, and ugly litter and fragments. It is the flies which find these gardens pleasant. Theirs is now the only voice of Summer, as though they were loathly in the mouth of Summer's carcase. It is perplexing to find how little remains of the common things of the household a broken doll, a child's boot, a trampled bonnet. Once in such a town I found a corn-chandler's ledger.

6   It was lying open in the muck of the roadway, wet and discoloured. Till that moment I had not come to the point of believing the place. The town was not humane. It was not credible. It might have been, for all I could tell, a simulacrum of the work of men. Perhaps it was the patient and particular mimicry of us by an unknown

power, a power which was alarmingly interested in our doings and in a frenzy over its partial failure it had attempted to demolish its laborious semblance of what we do. Was this power still observant of its work, and conscious of intruders? All this was a sinister warning of something invisible and malign, which brooded over our affairs, knew us too well, though omitting the heart of us, and it was mocking us now by defiling in an inhuman rage its own caricature of our appearance.

7   But there, lying in the road, was that corn-chandler's ledger. It was the first understandable thing I had seen that day. I began to believe these abandoned and silent ruins had lived and flourished, had once a warm kindred life moving in their empty chambers; enclosed a comfortable community, like placid Casterbridge. Men did stand here on sunny market days, and sorted wheat in the hollows of their hands. And with all that wide and hideous disaster of the Somme around it was suddenly understood (as when an essential light at home, but a light that has been casually valued, goes out, and leaves you to the dark) that an elderly farmer, looking for the best seed corn in the market-place, while his daughter the dairymaid is flirting with his neighbour's son, are more to us than all the Importances and the Great Ones who in all history till now have proudly and expertly tended their culture of discords.

8   I don't know that I ever read a book with more interest than that corn-chandler's ledger; though at one time, when it was merely a commonplace record of the common life which circulated there, testifying to its industry and the response of earth, it would have been no matter to me. Not for such successes are our flags displayed and our bells set pealing. It named customers at Thiepval, Martinpuich, Courcelette, Combles, Longueval, Contalmaison, Pozières, Guillemont, Montauban. It was not easy to understand it, my knowledge of those places being what it was. Those villages did not exist, except as corruption in a land that was tumbled into waves of glistening clay where the bodies of men were rotting disregarded

like those of dogs sprawled on a midden. My knowledge of that country, got with some fatigue, anxiety, fright, and on certain days dull contempt for the worst that could happen, because it seemed that nothing could matter any more, my idea of that country was such that the contrast of those ledger accounts was uncanny and unbelievable. Yet amid all the misery and horror of the Somme, with its shattering reminder of finality and futility at every step whichever way you turned, that ledger in the road, with none to read it, was the gospel promising that life should rise again; the suggestion of a forgotten but surviving virtue which would return, and cover the dread we knew, till a ploughman of the future would stop at rare relics, holding them up to the sun, and dimly recall ancient tales of woe.

» (1922)

The Derelict

H. M. Tomlinson

1   In a tramp steamer, which was overloaded, and in midwinter, I had
     crossed to America for the first time. What we experienced of the
     western ocean during that passage gave me so much respect for it
     that the prospect of the return journey, three thousand miles of
     those seas between me and home, was already a dismal foreboding.

2   The shipping posters of New York, showing stately liners too lofty
     even to notice the Atlantic, were arguments good enough for steer-
     age passengers, who do, I know, reckon a steamer's worth by the
     number of its funnels; but the pictures did nothing to lessen my
     regard for that dark outer world I knew. And having no experience
     of ships installed with racquet courts, Parisian cafes, swimming
     baths, and pergolas, I was naturally puzzled by the inconsequential
     behavior of the first-class passengers at the hotel. They were leaving
     by the liner which was to take me, and, I gathered, were going to
     cross a bridge to England in the morning. Of course, this might
     have been merely the innocent profanity of the simple-minded.

3   Embarking at the quay next day, I could not see that our ship had
     either a beginning or an end. There was a blank wall which ran out
     of sight to the right and left. How far it went, and what it enclosed,
     were beyond me. Hundreds of us in a slow procession mounted
     stairs to the upper floor of a warehouse, and from thence a bridge
     led us to a door in the wall half-way in its height. No funnels could
     be seen. Looking straight up from the embarkation gangway, along
     what seemed the parapet of the wall was a row of far-off indistin-
     guishable faces peering straight down at us. There was no evidence
     that this building we were entering, of which the high black wall
     was a part, was not an important and permanent feature of the city.
     It was in keeping with the magnitude of New York's skyscrapers,
     which this planet's occasionally non-irritant skin permits to stand

there to afford man an apparent reason to be gratified with his own capacity and daring.

4   But with the knowledge that this wall must be afloat there came no sense of security when, going through that little opening in its altitude, I found myself in a spacious decorated interior which hinted nothing of a ship, for I was puzzled as to direction. My last ship could be surveyed in two glances; she looked, and was, a comprehensible ship, no more than a manageable handful for an able master. In that ship you could see at once where you were and what to do. But in this liner you could not see where you were, and would never know which way to take unless you had a good memory. No understanding came to me in that hall of a measured and shapely body, designed with a cunning informed by ages of sea-lore to move buoyantly and surely among the raging seas, to balance delicately, a quick and sensitive being, to every precarious slope, to recover a lost poise easily and with the grace natural to a quick creature controlled by an alert mind.

5   There was no shape at all to this structure. I could see no line the run of which gave me warrant that it was comprised in the rondure of a ship. The lines were all of straight corridors, which, for all I knew, might have ended blindly on open space, as streets which traverse a city and are bare in vacancy beyond the dwellings. It was possible we were encompassed by walls, but only one wall was visible. There we idled, all strangers, in a large hall roofed by a dome of colored glass. Quite properly, palms stood beneath. There were offices and doors everywhere. On a broad staircase a multitude of us wandered aimlessly up and down. Each side of the stairway were electric lifts, intermittent and brilliant apparitions. I began to understand why the saloon passengers thought nothing of the voyage. They were encountering nothing unfamiliar. They had but come to another hotel for a few days.

6   I attempted to find my cabin, but failed. A uniformed guide took care of me. But my cabin, curtained, upholstered, and warm, with

mirrors and plated ware, sunk somewhere deeply among carpeted and silent streets down each of which the perspective of glow-lamps looked interminable, left me still questioning. The long walk had given me a fear that I was remote from important affairs which might be happening beyond. My address was 323. The street door—I was down a side turning, though—bore that number. A visitor could make no mistake, supposing he could find the street and my side turning. That was it. There was a very great deal in this place for everybody to remember, and most of us were strangers. No doubt, however, we were afloat, if the lifebelts in the rack meant anything. Yet the cabin, insulated from all noise, was not soothing, but disturbing. I had been used to a ship in which you could guess all that was happening even when in your bunk; a sensitive and communicative ship.

7   A steward appeared at my door, a stranger out of nowhere, and asked whether I had seen a bag not mine in the cabin. He might have been created merely to put that question, for I never saw him again on the voyage. This liner was a large province having irregular and shifting bounds, permitting incontinent entrance and disappearance. All this should have inspired me with an idea of our vastness and importance, but it did not. I felt I was one of a multitude included in a nebulous mass too vague to hold together unless we were constantly wary.

8   In the saloon there was the solid furniture of rare woods, the ornate decorations, and the light and shadows making vague its limits and giving it an appearance of immensity, to keep the mind from the thought of our real circumstances. At dinner we had valen-tine music, dreamy stuff to accord with the shaded lamps which displayed the tables in a lower rosy light. It helped to extend the mysterious and romantic shadows. The pale, disembodied masks of the waiters swam in the dusk above the tinted light. I had for a companion a vivacious American lady from the Middle West, and she looked round that prospect we had of an expensive cafe, and

said, "Well, but I am disappointed. Why, I've been looking forward to seeing the ocean, you know. And it isn't here."

9   "Smooth passage," remarked a man on the other side. "No sea at all worth mentioning." Actually, I know there was a heavy beam sea running before a half-gale. I could guess the officer in charge somewhere on the exposed roof might have another mind about it; but it made no difference to us in our circle of rosy intimate light bound by those vague shadows which were alive with ready servitude.

10   "And I've been reading Captains Courageous with this voyage in view. Isn't this the month when the forties roar? I want to hear them roar, just once, you know, and as gently as any sucking dove." We all laughed. "We can't even tell we're in a ship."

11   She began to discuss Kipling's book. "There's some fine seas in that. Have you read it? But I'd like to know where that ocean is he pretends to have seen. I do believe the realists are no more reliable than the romanticists. Here we are a thousand miles out, and none of us has seen the sea yet. Tell me, does not a realist have to magnify his awful billows just to get them into his reader's view?"

12   I murmured something feeble and sociable. I saw then why sailors never talk directly of the sea. I, for instance, could not find my key at that moment—it was in another pocket somewhere—so I had no iron to touch. Talking largely of the sea is something like the knowing talk of young men about women; and what is a simple sailor man that he should open his mouth on mysteries?

13   Only on the liner's boat-deck, where you could watch her four funnels against the sky, could you see to what extent the liner was rolling. The arc seemed to be considerable then, but slowly described. But the roll made little difference to the promenaders below. Sometimes they walked a short distance on the edges of their boots, leaning over as they did so, and swerving from the straight, as though they had turned giddy. The shadows formed by

the weak sunlight moved slowly out of ambush across the white deck, but often moved indecisively, as though uncertain of a need to go; and then slowly went into hiding again. The sea whirling and leaping past was far below our wall side. It was like peering dizzily over a precipice when watching those green and white cataracts.

14 The passengers, wrapped and comfortable on the lee deck, chatted as blithely as at a garden-party, while the band played medleys of national airs to suit our varied complexions. The stewards came round with loaded trays. A diminutive and wrinkled dame in costly furs frowned through her golden spectacles at her book, while her maid sat attentively by. An American actress was the center of an eager group of grinning young men; she was unseen, but her voice was distinct. The two Vanderbilts took their brisk constitutional among us as though the liner had but two real passengers though many invisible nobodies. The children, who had not ceased laughing and playing since we left New York, waited for the slope of the deck to reach its greatest, and then ran down toward the bulwarks precipitously. The children, happy and innocent, completed for us the feeling of comfortable indifference and security which we found when we saw there was more ship than ocean. The liner's deck canted slowly to leeward, went over more and more, beyond what it had done yet, and a pretty little girl with dark curls riotous from under her red tam-o'shanter, ran down, and brought up against us violently with both hands, laughing heartily. We laughed too. Looking seaward, I saw receding the broad green hill, snow-capped, which had lifted us and let us down. The sea was getting up.

15 Near sunset, when the billows were mounting express along our run, sometimes to leap and snatch at our upper structure, and were rocking us with some ease, there was a commotion forward. Books and shawls went anywhere as the passengers ran. Something strange was to be seen upon the waters.

16 It looked like a big log out there ahead, over the starboard bow.

It was not easy to make out. The light was failing. We overhauled it rapidly, and it began to shape as a ship's boat. "Oh, it's gone," exclaimed someone then. But the forlorn object lifted high again, and sank once more. Whenever it was glimpsed it was set in a patch of foam.

17 That flotsam, whatever it was, was of man. As we watched it intently, and before it was quite plain, we knew intuitively that hope was not there, that we were watching something past its doom. It drew abeam, and we saw what it was, a derelict sailing ship, mastless and awash. The alien wilderness was around us now, and we saw a sky that was overcast and driven, and seas that were uplifted, which had grown incredibly huge, swift, and perilous, and they had colder and more somber hues.

18 The derelict was a schooner, a lifeless and soddened hulk, so heavy and uncontesting that its foundering seemed at hand. The waters poured back and forth at her waist, as though holding her body captive for the assaults of the active seas which came over her broken bulwarks, and plunged ruthlessly about. There was something ironic in the indifference of her defenseless body to these unending attacks. It mocked this white and raging post-mortem brutality, and gave her a dignity that was cold and superior to all the eternal powers could now do. She pitched helplessly head first into a hollow, and a door flew open under the break of her poop; it surprised and shocked us, for the dead might have signed to us then. She went astern of us fast, and a great comber ran at her, as if it had but just spied her, and thought she was escaping. There was a high white flash, and a concussion we heard. She had gone. But she appeared again far away, on a summit in desolation, black against the sunset. The stump of her bowsprit, the accusatory finger of the dead, pointed at the sky.

19 I turned, and there beside me was the lady who had wanted to find the sea. She was gazing at the place where the wreck was last seen,

her eyes fixed, her mouth a little open in awe and horror.

»   (1922)

A First Impression

H. M. Tomlinson

1   Certainly it was an inconsiderate way of approaching the greatest city of the Americas, but that was not my fault. I wished for the direct approach, the figure of Liberty to rise, haughty and most calm, a noble symbol, as we came in from overseas; then the wide portals; then New York. But the erratic tracks of a tramp steamer, however, go not as her voyagers will. They have no control over her. She moves to an enigmatic will in London. It happens, then, that she rarely shows a wonder of the world any respect. She arrives like sudden rain, like wind from a new quarter. She is as chance as the fall of a star. None knows the day nor the hour. At the most inconvenient time she takes the wonder's visitors to the back door.

2   We went, light ship from the South, to Barbados, for orders; and because I wanted New York, for that was the way home, we were sent to Tampa for phosphates. As to Tampa, its position on the globe is known only to underwriters and shipbrokers; it is that sort of place. It is a mere name, like Fernando de Noronha, or Key West, which one meets only in the shipping news, idly wondering then what strange things the seafarer would find if he went.

3   Late one night, down a main street of Tampa, there came, with the deliberate movement of fate, a gigantic corridor train, looming as high as a row of lighted villas, and drawn by the awful engine of a dream. That train behaved there as trains do at home, presently stopping alongside a foot-way.

4   Behind me was a little wooden shop. In front was the wall of a carriage, having an entrance on the second storey, and a roof athwart the meridian stars. One of its wheels was the nearest and most dominant object in the night to me, a monstrous bright round resting on a muddy newspaper in the road. It absorbed all the light from the little wooden shop. Now, I had hunted through-

out Tampa for its railway terminus, fruitlessly; but here its train had found me, keeping me from crossing the road.

5   "Where do I board this train for New York?" I asked. (I talked like a fool, I know; it was like asking a casual wayfarer in East Ham whether that by the kerb is the Moscow express. Yet what was I to do?) "Board her right here," said the fellow, who was in his shirt sleeves. Therefore I delivered myself, in blind faith, to the casual gods who are apt to wake up and by a series of deft little miracles get things done fitly in America when all seems lost and the travel- ler has even bared his resigned neck to the stroke.

6   But I had not the least hope of seeing New York and a Cunarder; not with such an unpropitious start as that. With an exit like Euston one never doubts sure direction, and arrival at the precise spot at the exact moment. You feel there it was arranged for in Genesis. The officials cannot alter affairs. They are priests admin- istering inviolate rites, advancing matters fore-ordained by the unseen, and so no more able to stay or speed this cosmic concern than the astronomer who schedules the planets. The planets take their heavenly courses. But I had never been to the United States before, did not know even the names of their many gods, and New York was at the end of a great journey; and the train for it stopped outside a tobacco shop in the road, like a common tram.

7   There was another night when, with the usual unreason, the swift and luxurious glide, lessening through easy gradations, ceased. I saw some lights in the rain outside. How should I know it was New York? We had even changed climates since we started. The passengers of my early days in the train had passed away. There was nothing to show. More, I felt no exultation—which should have been the first of warnings. Merely we got to a railway station one night, and a negro insisted that I should get out and stop out. This was Noo Yark, he said.

8   It was night, I repeat; there was a row of cabs in a dolorous rain. I saw a man in a shiny cape under the nearest lamp, and beyond him

a vista of reflections from vacant stones, which to me always, more than bleak hills or the empty round of the sea, is desolation. There were no spacious portals. There was no figure of Liberty, haughty but welcoming. There was rain, and cabs that waited without hope. There was exactly what you find at the end of a twopenny journey when your only luggage is an evening paper, an umbrella, and that tired feeling. Not knowing where to go, and little caring, I followed the crowd, and so found myself in a large well-lighted hall. Having no business there—it was a barren place—I pushed on, and came suddenly to the rim of the world.

9   Before me was the immensity of dark celestial space in which wandered hosts of uncharted stars; and below my feet was the abyss of old night. Just behind me was a woman telling her husband that they had forgotten Jimmy's boots, and couldn't go back now, for the ferry was just coming.

10 Jimmy's boots! Now, when you are a released soul, ascending the night, and the earth below is a bright silver ball, not so very big, and some other viewless soul behind you, still with thoughts absent on worldly trifles, mutters concerning boots when in the Milky Way, you will know how I felt. Here was the ultimate empty dark in which the sun could never shine. The sun had not merely left the place. It had never been there. It was a remote star, one of myriads in the constellations at large, the definite groups which occulted in the void before me. Looking at those swiftly moving systems, I watched for the flash of impact; but no great light of collision broke. The groups of lights passed and repassed noiselessly.

11 Then one constellation presently detached itself, and its orbit evidently would intersect our foothold. It came nearer out of the night, till I could see plainly that it appeared to be a long section of a well-lighted street, say, like a length of Piccadilly. It approached end-on to where I stood, and at last impinged. It actually was a length of street, and I could continue my walk. The street floated off again into the night, with me, Jimmy's father and mother, and

all of us, and the vans and motor-cars; and the other square end of it soon joined a roadway on the opposite shore. The dark river was as full of mobile lengths of bright roadway as Oxford Circus is of motor-buses; and the fear of the unknown, as in the terrific dark of a dream where flaming comets stream on undirected courses, numbed my little mind. I had found New York.

12 I had found it. Its bulk was beyond the mind, its lights were falling star systems, and its movements those of general cataclysm. I should find no care for little human needs there. One cannot warm one's hands against the flames of earthquake. There is no provision for men in the welter, but dimly apprehended in the night, of blind and inhuman powers.

13 Therefore, the hotel bedroom, when I got to it, surprised and steadied me with its elaborate care for the body. But yet I was not certain. Then I saw against the wall a dial, and reading a notice over it I learned that by working the hands of this false clock correctly I could procure anything, from an apple to the fire brigade. Now this was carrying matters to the other extreme; and I had to suppress a desire to laugh hysterically. I set the hands to a number; waited one minute; then the door opened, and a waiter came in with a real tray, conveying a glass and a bottle. So there was a method then in this general madness after all. I tried to regard the wonder as indifferently as the waiter's own cold and measuring eyes.

» (1922)

Binding a Spell

H. M. Tomlinson

1   You may never have addressed a meeting of the public, but you have long cherished a vision of a figure (well known to your private mirror) standing where it overlooks an intent and silent multitude to which it communicates with apt and fluent words those things not seen by mortal eyes, the dream of a world not ours... . You know what I mean. (Loud and prolonged applause.)

2   "I should be glad," wrote one who is still unashamed to call himself my friend, "if you could run down here one evening and address a meeting on your experiences. Just conversationally, you know."

3   A casual sort of letter. Designedly so. But I could see through it. It was an invitation which did not wish to scare me from accepting it. I smiled with serene amusement at its concluding sentence. Conversationally! Why, that would be merely talking; tongue-work; keeping on and on after one usually, if merciful to a friend, lets him off. I felt instantly that for once it might be even more pleasant to entertain an audience than to be one of the crowd and bored. And it happened that my experiences really did give me something to say, and were exactly what an audience, in war-time, might be glad to hear. I therefore wrote a brief note of acceptance, as one to whom this sort of thing comes ten times a day; and thought no more about it.

4   No more, that is to say, till I saw the local paper announced me as a coming event, a treat in store. I was on the list. There were those that evening who, instead of going to a theatre, a concert, or to see Vesta Tilley, would come to hear me. I felt then the first cold underdraught of doubt, the chilling intimation from the bleak unknown, where it is your own affair entirely whether you flourish or perish. What a draught! I got up, shut the door, and looked at the day of the month.

5   That was all right; yet another fortnight!

6   But what weakness was this? Anybody could do it, if they knew as much of my subject as did I. Many men would do it, without a tremor, without shame, if they knew next to nothing about it. Look at old Brown, for example, whose only emotions are evoked by being late for dinner, the price of building materials, the scandalous incapacity of workmen, and the restriction of the liberty of the subject by trade unions! He will sit, everybody knows, while wearing plaid trousers and side-whiskers, on the right hand of a peer, in full view of thousands, at a political meeting, untroubled, bland, conscious of his worth, and will rise at the word, thumbs carelessly thrust into his waistcoat pockets, begin with a jest (the same one), and for an hour make aspirates as uncommon as are bathrooms in his many houses.

7   He has nothing to say, and could not say it if he had; but he can speak in public. You will observe the inference is obvious. One who is really capable of constructive thought (like you and me); who has a wide range of words to choose from even when running; who is touched, by events, to admiration, to indignation, to alarm, to—to all that sort of thing, he could … the plastic audience would be in his skilful hands, there is no doubt. (Hear, hear!)

8   Time passed. As Mr. A. Ward once pointed out, it is a way time has. The night came, as at last I began to fear it would. My brief notes were in my pocket, for I had resolutely put from me the dishonourable and barren safety of a written lecture. In the train—how cold was the night—I wished I had gone more fully into the matter. Slightly shivering, I tried to recall the dry humour of those carefully prepared opening sentences which shortly would prove to my audience that I had their measure, and was at ease; would prove that my elevation on the platform was not merely through four feet of deal planking, but was a real overlooking. But those delicate sentences had broken somehow. They were shards, and not a glitter of humour was sticking to the fragments.

9   I felt I would rather again approach one of those towns in France, where it was likely you would run into the Uhlans, than go to that lecture hall. No doubt, too, my friend had explained to them what a clever fellow I was, in order to get some reflected glory out of it. Then it would serve him right; there would be two of us.

10 The hall was nearly full. What surprises one is to find so many ladies present. A most disquieting fact, entirely unforeseen. They sit in the front rows and wait, evidently in a tranquil, alert, and mirthful mind, for you to begin. I could hear their leisurely converse and occasional subdued laughter (about what?) even where, in a sort of frozen, lucid calm, indifferent to my fate, the mood of all Englishmen in moments of extreme peril, I was handing my hat and coat to my friend in a room behind the platform. All those people out there were waiting for me.

11 When we got on the platform the chairman told them something about me, I don't know what, but when I looked up it was to find, like the soul in torment, that a multitude of bodiless eyes had fixed me—eyes intent, curious, passionless.

12 "I call upon——" said the chairman.

13 I stood up. The sound of my voice uplifted in that silence was the most startling sound I have ever heard. Shortly after that there came the paralysing discovery that it is a gift to be able to think while hundreds wait patiently to see what the thought is like when it comes. This made my brow hot. There was a boy in an Eton suit, sitting in front with his legs wide apart, who was grinning at me through his spectacles. How he got there I don't know. I think he was the gift of the gods. His smile so annoyed me that I forgot myself, which saved me. I just talked to that boy.

14 Once there was loud laughter. Why? It is inexplicable. I talked for about an hour. About what? Heaven knows. The chairman kindly let me out through a side entrance.

»   (1922)

Lent

H. M. Tomlinson

1   It was Meredith's country, and Atlantic weather in Lent. The downs were dilated and clear as though seen through crystal. A far company of pines on the high skyline were magnified into delicate inky figures. The vacant sward below them was as lucent as the slope of a vast approaching wave. A blackbird was fluting after a shower, for the sky was transient blue with the dark rags of the squall flying fast over the hill towards London. The thatched roof of a cottage in the valley suddenly flamed with a light of no earthly fire, as though a god had arrived, and that was the sign. Miss Muffet, whose profile, having the breeze and the surprise of the sun in her hair, was dedicated with a quivering and aureate nimbus, pulled aside the brush of a small yew, and exclaimed; for there, neatly set in the angle of the bough, was a brown cup with three blue eggs in it. I saw all this, and tried my best to get back to it; but I was not there. I saw it clearly—the late shower glittered on my coat and on the yew with the nest in it—but it was a scene remote as a memorable hour of a Surrey April of years ago. I could not approach; so I went back into the house.

2   But there was no escape. For I freely own that I am one of those who refused to believe there would be "a great offensive." (Curse such trite and sounding words, which put measureless misery through the mind as unconsciously as a boy repeats something of Euclid.) I believed that no man would now dare to order it. The soldiers, I knew, with all the signs before them, still could not credit that it would be done. The futile wickedness of these slaughters had been proved too often. They get nowhere. They settle nothing. This last, if it came, would be worse than all the rest in its magnitude and horror; it would deprive Europe of a multitude more of our diminishing youth, and end, in the exhaustion of its impetus, with peace no nearer than before. The old and indurated Importances in

authority, safe far behind the lines, would shrink from squandering humanity's remaining gold of its life, even though their ignoble ends were yet unachieved. But it had been ordered. Age, its blind jealousy for control now stark mad, impotent in all but the will and the power to command and punish, ignoring every obvious lesson of the past, the appeal of the tortured for the sun again and leisure even to weep, and the untimely bones of the young as usual now as flints in the earth of Europe, had deliberately put out the glimmer of dawn.

3 Well for those who may read the papers without personal knowledge of what happens when such a combat has begun; but to know, and to be useless; to be looking with that knowledge at Meredith's country in radiant April! There are occasions, though luckily they come but once or twice in life, when the mind is shocked by the basal verities apparently moving as though they were fugitive; thought becomes dizzy at the daylight earth suddenly falling away at one's feet to the vacuity of the night. Some choice had to be made. I recalled another such mental convulsion by Amiens Cathedral, near midnight, nearly four years ago, with the French guns rumbling through the city in retreat, and the certainty that the enemy would be there by morning on his way to Paris. One thing a campaigner learns that matters are rarely quite so bad or so good as they seem. Saying this to my friend, the farmer (who replied that, in any case, he must go and look to the cows), I turned to some books.

4 Yet resolution is needed to get the thoughts indoors at such a time. They are out of command. A fire is necessary. You must sit beside a company of flames leaping from a solidly established fire, flames curling out of the lambent craters of a deep centre; and steadily look into that. After a while your hand goes out slowly for the book. It has become acceptable. You have got your thoughts home. They were of no use in France, dwelling upon those villages and cross-roads you once knew, now spouting smoke and flames, where

good friends are waiting, having had their last look on earth, as the doomed rearguards.

5   The best books for refuge in times of stress are of the "notebook" and "table-talk" kind. Poetry I have tried, but could not approach it. It is too distant. Romance, which many found good, would never hold my attention. But I had Samuel Butler's Note Books with me for two years in France, and found that the right sort of thing. You may begin anywhere. There are no threads to look for. And you may stop for a time, while some strange notion of the author's is in contest for the command of the intelligence with your dark, resurgent thoughts; but Butler always won. His mental activity is too fibrous, masculine, and unexpected for any nonsense. But I had to keep a sharp eye on Butler. His singular merits were discovered by others who had no more than heard of him, but found he was exactly what they wanted. If his volume of Note Books is not the best example of its sort we have, then I should be glad to learn the name of the best. This Lent I tried Coleridge again. But surely one's mind must be curiously at random to go to such wool-gathering. I found him what I fear Lamb and his friends knew him to be—a tireless and heavy preacher through the murk of whose nebulous scholarship and philosophy the revealing gleams of wisdom are so rare that you are almost too weary to open the eyes to them when they flash. Selden is better, but abstract, legal, and dry.

6   Hazlitt compelled a renewal of an old respect; his humanity, his instinct for essentials, his cool detection of pretence and cant, however finely disguised, and his English with its frank love for the embodying noun and the active verb, make reading very like the clear, hard, bright, vigorous weather of the downs when the wind is up-Channel. It is bracing. But I discovered another notebook, of which I have heard so little that it shows what good things may be lost in war; for this book was published in 1914. It is the Impressions and Comments of Havelock Ellis. There have been in the past critics of life and the things men do who have been

observers as acute, as well-equipped in knowledge, and have had a command of English as free and accurate, as the author of Impressions and Comments; but not many. Yet such judgments of men, their affairs and their circumstances, could have been written in no other time than the years just before the war—the first note is dated July 1912. The reflections are often chill and exposed; but so is a faithful mirror bleak, though polished and gleaming, when held up to grey affairs in the light of a day which is ominous. You seem to feel in this book the cold draught moving before the storm which has not come—the author knew of no storm to come, and does not even hint at it; but the portents, and the look of the minds of his fellows, make him feel uncomfortable, and he asks what ails us. Now we know. It is strange that a book so wise and enlivening, whether it is picturing the Cornish coast in spring, the weakness of peace propaganda, Bianca Stella, Rabelais, the Rules of Art, the Bayeux Tapestry, or Spanish cathedrals, should have been mislaid and forgotten. . . .

7   The fire is dying. It is grey, fallen, and cold. The house is late and silent. There is no sound but the ghostly creaking of a stair; our thoughts are stealing away again. We creep out after them to the outer gate. What are books and opinions? The creakings of an old house uneasy with the heavy remembrances and the melancholy of antiquity, and with some midnight presage of its finality.

8   The wind and rain have passed. There is now but the icy stillness and quiet of outer space. The earth is Limbo, the penumbra of a dark and partial recollection; the shadow, vague and dawnless, over a vast stage from which the consequential pageant has gone, and is almost forgotten, the memory of many events merged now into formless night itself, and foundered profoundly beneath the glacial brilliance of a clear heaven alive with stars. Only the stars live, and only the stars overlook the place that was ours. The war—was there a war? It must have been long ago. Perhaps the shades are troubled with vestiges of an old and dreadful sin. If once there

were men who heard certain words, and became spellbound, and in the impulse of that madness forgot that their earth was good, but very brief, and turned from their children and women and the cherished work of their hands to slay each other and destroy their communities, it all happened just as the leaves of an autumn that is gone once fell before the sudden mania of a wind, and are resolved. What year was that? The leaves of an autumn that is long past are beyond time. The night is their place, and only the unknowing stars look down to the little blot of midnight which was us, and our pride, and our wisdom, and our heroics.

»   (1922)

Bed-books and Night-lights

H. M. Tomlinson

1   The rain flashed across the midnight window with a myriad feet.
There was a groan in outer darkness, the Voice of all nameless
dreads. The nervous candle-flame shuddered by my bedside. The
groaning rose to a shriek, and the little flame jumped in a panic,
and nearly left its white column. Out of the corners of the room
swarmed the released shadows. Black spectres danced in ecstasy
over my bed. I love fresh air, but I cannot allow it to slay the shining
and delicate body of my little friend the candle-flame, the comrade
who ventures with me into the solitudes beyond midnight. I shut
the window.

2   They talk of the candle-power of an electric bulb. What do they
mean? It cannot have the faintest glimmer of the real power of
my candle. It would be as right to express, in the same inverted
and foolish comparison, the worth of "those delicate sisters, the
Pleiades." That pinch of star dust, the Pleiades, exquisitely remote
in deepest night, in the profound where light all but fails, has
not the power of a sulphur match; yet, still apprehensive to the
mind though dimmering on the limit of vision, and sometimes
even vanishing, it brings into distinction those distant and difficult tints—hidden far behind all our verified thoughts—which we
rarely properly view. I should like to know of any great arc-lamp
which could do that. So the star-like candle for me. No other light
follows so intimately an author's most ghostly suggestion. We sit,
the candle and I, in the midst of the shades we are conquering, and
sometimes look up from the lucent page to contemplate the dark
hosts of the enemy with a smile before they overwhelm us as they
will, of course. Like me, the candle is mortal; it will burn out.

3   As the bed-book itself should be a sort of night-light, to assist its
illumination, coarse lamps are useless. They would douse the book.

The light for such a book must accord with it. It must be, like the book, a limited, personal, mellow, and companionable glow; the solitary taper beside the only worshipper in a sanctuary. That is why nothing can compare with the intimacy of candle-light for a bed-book. It is a living heart, bright and warm in central night, burning for us alone, holding the gaunt and towering shadows at bay. There the monstrous spectres stand in our midnight room, the advance guard of the darkness of the world, held off by our valiant little glim, but ready to flood instantly and founder us in original gloom.

4　The wind moans without; ancient evils are at large and wandering in torment. The rain shrieks across the window. For a moment, for just a moment, the sentinel candle is shaken, and burns blue with terror. The shadows leap out instantly. The little flame recovers, and merely looks at its foe the darkness, and back to its own place goes the old enemy of light and man. The candle for me, tiny, mortal, warm, and brave, a golden lily on a silver stem.

5　"Almost any book does for a bed-book," a woman once said to me. I nearly replied in a hurry that almost any woman would do for a wife; but that is not the way to bring people to conviction of sin. Her idea was that the bed-book is a soporific, and for that reason she even advocated the reading of political speeches. That would be a dissolute act. Certainly you would go to sleep; but in what a frame of mind. You would enter into sleep with your eyes shut. It would be like dying, not only unshriven, but in the act of guilt.

6　What book shall it shine upon? Think of Plato, or Dante, or Tolstoy, or a Blue Book, for such an occasion I cannot. They will not do—they are no good to me. I am not writing about you. I know those men I have named are transcendent, the greater lights. But I am bound to confess at times they bore me. Though their feet are clay and on earth, just as ours, their stellar brows are sometimes dim in remote clouds. For my part, they are too big for bedfellows. I cannot see myself, carrying my feeble and restricted glim, following (in pyjamas) the statuesque figure of the Florentine where it stalks, aloof in its garb of austere pity, the sonorous deeps of Hades. Hades! Not for me; not after midnight! Let those go who like it.

7   As for the Russian, vast and disquieting, I refuse to leave all, including the blankets and the pillow, to follow him into the gelid tranquillity of the upper air, where even the colours are prismatic spicules of ice, to brood upon the erratic orbit of the poor mud-ball below called earth. I know it is my world also; but I cannot help that. It is too late, after a busy day, and at that hour, to begin overtime on fashioning a new and better planet out of cosmic dust. By breakfast-time, nothing useful would have been accomplished. We should all be where we were the night before. The job is far too long, once the pillow is nicely set.

8   For the truth is, there are times when we are too weary to remain attentive and thankful under the improving eye, kindly but severe, of the seers. There are times when we do not wish to be any better than we are. We do not wish to be elevated and improved. At midnight, away with such books! As for the literary pundits, the high priests of the Temple of Letters, it is interesting and helpful occasionally for an acolyte to swinge them a good hard one with an incense-burner, and cut and run, for a change, to something outside their rubrics. Midnight is the time when one can recall, with ribald delight, the names of all the Great Works which every gentleman ought to have read, but which some of us have not. For there is almost as much clotted nonsense written about literature as there is about theology.

9   There are few books which go with midnight, solitude, and a candle. It is much easier to say what does not please us then than what is exactly right. The book must be, anyhow, something benedictory by a sinning fellow-man. Cleverness would be repellent at such an hour. Cleverness, anyhow, is the level of mediocrity to-day we are all too infernally clever. The first witty and perverse paradox blows out the candle. Only the sick in mind crave cleverness, as

a morbid body turns to drink. The late candle throws its beams a great distance; and its rays make transparent much that seemed massy and important. The mind at rest beside that light, when the house is asleep, and the consequential affairs of the urgent world have diminished to their right proportions because we see them distantly from another and a more tranquil place in the heavens where duty, honour, witty arguments, controversial logic on great questions, appear such as will leave hardly a trace of fossil in the indurated mud which presently will cover them—the mind then certainly smiles at cleverness.

10 For though at that hour the body may be dog-tired, the mind is white and lucid, like that of a man from whom a fever has abated. It is bare of illusions. It has a sharp focus, small and star-like, as a clear and lonely flame left burning by the altar of a shrine from which all have gone but one. A book which approaches that light in the privacy of that place must come, as it were, with honest and open pages.

11 I like Heine then, though. His mockery of the grave and great, in those sentences which are as brave as pennants in a breeze, is comfortable and sedative. One's own secret and awkward convictions, never expressed because not lawful and because it is hard to get words to bear them lightly, seem then to be heard aloud in the mild, easy, and confident diction of an immortal whose voice has the blitheness of one who has watched, amused and irreverent, the high gods in eager and secret debate on the best way to keep the gilt and trappings on the body of the evil they have created.

12 That first-rate explorer, Gulliver, is also fine in the light of the intimate candle. Have you read lately again his Voyage to the Houyhnhnms? Try it alone again in quiet. Swift knew all about our contemporary troubles. He has got it all down. Why was he called a misanthrope? Reading that last voyage of Gulliver in the select intimacy of midnight I am forced to wonder, not at Swift's hatred of mankind, not at his satire of his fellows, not at the strange

and terrible nature of this genius who thought that much of us, but how it is that after such a wise and sorrowful revealing of the things we insist on doing, and our reasons for doing them, and what happens after we have done them, men do not change. It does seem impossible that society could remain unaltered, after the surprise its appearance should have caused it as it saw its face in that ruthless mirror. We point instead to the fact that Swift lost his mind in the end. Well, that is not a matter for surprise.

13 Such books, and France's Isle of Penguins, are not disturbing as bed-books. They resolve one's agitated and outraged soul, relieving it with some free expression for the accusing and questioning thoughts engendered by the day's affairs. But they do not rest immediately to hand in the bookshelf by the bed. They depend on the kind of day one has had. Sterne is closer. One would rather be transported as far as possible from all the disturbances of earth's envelope of clouds, and Tristram Shandy is sure to be found in the sun.

14 But best of all books for midnight are travel books. Once I was lost every night for months with Doughty in the Arabia Deserta. He is a craggy author. A long course of the ordinary facile stuff, such as one gets in the Press, every day, thinking it is English, sends one thoughtless and headlong among the bitter herbs and stark boulders of Doughty's burning and spacious expanse; only to get bewildered, and the shins broken, and a great fatigue at first, in a strange land of fierce sun, hunger, glittering spar, ancient plutonic rock, and very Adam himself. But once you are acclimatised, and know the language—it takes time—there is no more London after dark, till, a wanderer returned from a forgotten land, you emerge from the interior of Arabia on the Red Sea coast again, feeling as though you had lost touch with the world you used to know. And if that doesn't mean good writing I know of no other test.

15 Because once there was a father whose habit it was to read with his boys nightly some chapters of the Bible—and cordially they hated

that habit of his—I have that Book too; though I fear I have it for no reason that he, the rigid old faithful, would be pleased to hear about. He thought of the future when he read the Bible; I read it for the past. The familiar names, the familiar rhythm of its words, its wonderful well-remembered stories of things long past,—like that of Esther, one of the best in English,—the eloquent anger of the prophets for the people then who looked as though they were alive, but were really dead at heart, all is solace and home to me. And now I think of it, it is our home and solace that we want in a bed-book.

» (1922)

Impressions of America

By Oscar Wilde

I.

LE JARDIN.

The lily's withered chalice falls
  Around its rod of dusty gold,
  And from the beech trees on the wold
The last wood-pigeon coos and calls.

The gaudy leonine sunflower
  Hangs black and barren on its stalk,
  And down the windy garden walk
The dead leaves scatter,--hour by hour.

Pale privet-petals white as milk
  Are blown into a snowy mass;
  The roses lie upon the grass,
Like little shreds of crimson silk.

II.

LA MER.

A white mist drifts across the shrouds,
  A wild moon in this wintry sky
  Gleams like an angry lion's eye
Out of a mane of tawny clouds.

The muffled steersman at the wheel

Is but a shadow in the gloom;--
And in the throbbing engine room
Leap the long rods of polished steel.

The shattered storm has left its trace
Upon this huge and heaving dome,
For the thin threads of yellow foam
Float on the waves like ravelled lace.

Oscar Wilde.

IMPRESSIONS OF AMERICA.

1   I fear I cannot picture America as altogether an Elysium--perhaps, from the ordinary standpoint I know but little about the country. I cannot give its latitude or longitude; I cannot compute the value of its dry goods, and I have no very close acquaintance with its politics. These are matters which may not interest you, and they certainly are not interesting to me.

2   The first thing that struck me on landing in America was that if the Americans are not the most well-dressed people in the world, they are the most comfortably dressed. Men are seen there with the dreadful chimney-pot hat, but there are very few hatless men; men wear the shocking swallow-tail coat, but few are to be seen with no coat at all. There is an air of comfort in the appearance of the people which is a marked contrast to that seen in this country, where, too often, people are seen in close contact with rags.

3   The next thing particularly noticeable is that everybody seems in a hurry to catch a train. This is a state of things which is not favourable to poetry or romance. Had Romeo or Juliet been in a constant state of anxiety about trains, or had their minds been agitated by the question of return-tickets, Shakespeare could not have given us those lovely balcony scenes which are so full of poetry and pathos.

4   America is the noisiest country that ever existed. One is waked up in the morning, not by the singing of the nightingale, but by the steam whistle. It is surprising that the sound practical sense of the Americans does not reduce this intolerable noise. All Art depends upon exquisite and delicate sensibility, and such continual turmoil must ultimately be destructive of the musical faculty.

5   There is not so much beauty to be found in American cities as in Oxford, Cambridge, Salisbury or Winchester, where are lovely relics of a beautiful age; but still there is a good deal of beauty to be seen in them now and then, but only where the American has not attempted to create it. Where the Americans have attempted to produce beauty they have signally failed. A remarkable characteristic of the Americans is the manner in which they have applied science to modern life.

6   This is apparent in the most cursory stroll through New York. In England an inventor is regarded almost as a crazy man, and in too many instances invention ends in disappointment and poverty. In America an inventor is honoured, help is forthcoming, and the exercise of ingenuity, the application of science to the work of man, is there the shortest road to wealth. There is no country in the world where machinery is so lovely as in America.

7   I have always wished to believe that the line of strength and the line of beauty are one. That wish was realised when I contemplated American machinery. It was not until I had seen the water-works at Chicago that I realised the wonders of machinery; the rise and fall of the steel rods, the symmetrical motion of the great wheels is the most beautifully rhythmic thing I have ever seen.[3] One is impressed in America, but not favourably impressed, by the inordinate size of everything. The country seems to try to bully one into a belief in its power by its impressive bigness.

8   I was disappointed with Niagara--most people must be disappointed with Niagara. Every American bride is taken there, and the sight of the stupendous waterfall must be one of the earliest, if not

the keenest, disappointments in American married life. One sees it under bad conditions, very far away, the point of view not showing the splendour of the water. To appreciate it really one has to see it from underneath the fall, and to do that it is necessary to be dressed in a yellow oil-skin, which is as ugly as a mackintosh--and I hope none of you ever wears one. It is a consolation to know, however, that such an artist as Madame Bernhardt has not only worn that yellow, ugly dress, but has been photographed in it.

9 Perhaps the most beautiful part of America is the West, to reach which, however, involves a journey by rail of six days, racing along tied to an ugly tin-kettle of a steam engine. I found but poor consolation for this journey in the fact that the boys who infest the cars and sell everything that one can eat--or should not eat--were selling editions of my poems vilely printed on a kind of grey blotting paper, for the low price of ten cents.[4] Calling these boys on one side I told them that though poets like to be popular they desire to be paid, and selling editions of my poems without giving me a profit is dealing a blow at literature which must have a disastrous effect on poetical aspirants. The invariable reply that they made was that they themselves made a profit out of the transaction and that was all they cared about.

10 It is a popular superstition that in America a visitor is invariably addressed as "Stranger." I was never once addressed as "Stranger." When I went to Texas I was called "Captain"; when I got to the centre of the country I was addressed as "Colonel," and, on arriving at the borders of Mexico, as "General." On the whole, however, "Sir," the old English method of addressing people is the most common.

11 It is, perhaps, worth while to note that what many people call Americanisms are really old English expressions which have lingered in our colonies while they have been lost in our own country. Many people imagine that the term "I guess," which is so common in America, is purely an American expression, but it was used by John

Locke in his work on "The Understanding," just as we now use "I think."[5]

12 It is in the colonies, and not in the mother country, that the old life of the country really exists. If one wants to realise what English Puritanism is--not at its worst (when it is very bad), but at its best, and then it is not very good--I do not think one can find much of it in England, but much can be found about Boston and Massachusetts. We have got rid of it. America still preserves it, to be, I hope, a short-lived curiosity.

13 San Francisco is a really beautiful city. China Town, peopled by Chinese labourers, is the most artistic town I have ever come across. The people--strange, melancholy Orientals, whom many people would call common, and they are certainly very poor--have determined that they will have nothing about them that is not beautiful. In the Chinese restaurant, where these navvies meet to have supper in the evening, I found them drinking tea out of china cups as delicate as the petals of a rose-leaf, whereas at the gaudy hotels I was supplied with a delf cup an inch and a half thick. When the Chinese bill was presented it was made out on rice paper, the account being done in Indian ink as fantastically as if an artist had been etching little birds on a fan.

14 Salt Lake City contains only two buildings of note, the chief being the Tabernacle, which is in the shape of a soup-kettle. It is decorated by the only native artist, and he has treated religious subjects in the naive spirit of the early Florentine painters, representing people of our own day in the dress of the period side by side with people of Biblical history who are clothed in some romantic costume.

15 The building next in importance is called the Amelia Palace, in honour of one of Brigham Young's wives. When he died the present president of the Mormons stood up in the Tabernacle and said that it had been revealed to him that he was to have the Amelia Palace, and that on this subject there were to be no more revelations of any kind!

16 From Salt Lake City one travels over the great plains of Colorado and up the Rocky Mountains, on the top of which is Leadville, the richest city in the world. It has also got the reputation of being the roughest, and every man carries a revolver. I was told that if I went there they would be sure to shoot me or my travelling manager. I wrote and told them that nothing that they could do to my travelling manager would intimidate me. They are miners--men working in metals, so I lectured to them on the Ethics of Art. I read them passages from the autobiography of Benvenuto Cellini and they seemed much delighted. I was reproved by my hearers for not having brought him with me. I explained that he had been dead for some little time which elicited the enquiry "Who shot him"? They afterwards took me to a dancing saloon where I saw the only rational method of art criticism I have ever come across. Over the piano was printed a notice:--

> PLEASE DO NOT SHOOT THE
> PIANIST.
> HE IS DOING HIS BEST.

17 The mortality among pianists in that place is marvellous. Then they asked me to supper, and having accepted, I had to descend a mine in a rickety bucket in which it was impossible to be graceful. Having got into the heart of the mountain I had supper, the first course being whisky, the second whisky and the third whisky.

18 I went to the Theatre to lecture and I was informed that just before I went there two men had been seized for committing a murder, and in that theatre they had been brought on to the stage at eight o'clock in the evening, and then and there tried and executed before a crowded audience. But I found these miners very charming and not at all rough.

19 Among the more elderly inhabitants of the South I found a melancholy tendency to date every event of importance by the late war. "How beautiful the moon is to-night," I once remarked to a gentleman who was standing next to me. "Yes," was his reply, "but you

should have seen it before the war."

20 So infinitesimal did I find the knowledge of Art, west of the Rocky Mountains, that an art patron--one who in his day had been a miner--actually sued the railroad company for damages because the plaster cast of Venus of Milo, which he had imported from Paris, had been delivered minus the arms. And, what is more surprising still, he gained his case and the damages.

21 Pennsylvania, with its rocky gorges and woodland scenery, reminded me of Switzerland. The prairie reminded me of a piece of blotting-paper.

22 The Spanish and French have left behind them memorials in the beauty of their names. All the cities that have beautiful names derive them from the Spanish or the French. The English people give intensely ugly names to places. One place had such an ugly name that I refused to lecture there. It was called Grigsville. Supposing I had founded a school of Art there--fancy "Early Grigsville." Imagine a School of Art teaching "Grigsville Renaissance."

23 As for slang I did not hear much of it, though a young lady who had changed her clothes after an afternoon dance did say that "after the heel kick she shifted her day goods."

24 American youths are pale and precocious, or sallow and supercilious, but American girls are pretty and charming--little oases of pretty unreasonableness in a vast desert of practical common-sense.

25 Every American girl is entitled to have twelve young men devoted to her. They remain her slaves and she rules them with charming nonchalance.

26 The men are entirely given to business; they have, as they say, their brains in front of their heads. They are also exceedingly acceptive of new ideas. Their education is practical. We base the education of children entirely on books, but we must give a child a mind before we can instruct the mind. Children have a natural antipathy to books--handicraft should be the basis of education. Boys and girls

should be taught to use their hands to make something, and they would be less apt to destroy and be mischievous.

27 In going to America one learns that poverty is not a necessary accompaniment to civilisation. There at any rate is a country that has no trappings, no pageants and no gorgeous ceremonies. I saw only two processions--one was the Fire Brigade preceded by the Police, the other was the Police preceded by the Fire Brigade.

28 Every man when he gets to the age of twenty-one is allowed a vote, and thereby immediately acquires his political education. The Americans are the best politically educated people in the world. It is well worth one's while to go to a country which can teach us the beauty of the word FREEDOM and the value of the thing LIBERTY.

» (1882)